LET JUSTICE & RIGHTEOUSNESS **PREVAIL**

Sermons and reflections for the pro-life Christian

Edited by Anna Nienhuis

Let Justice & Righteousness Prevail
Sermons and Reflections for the pro-life Christian
Copyright © 2021 by The Association for Reformed Political Action (ARPA) Canada
All rights reserved.

Library and Archives Canada Cataloguing in Publication

Title: Let justice & righteousness prevail : sermons and reflections for the pro-life Christian / edited by Anna Nienhuis.
Other titles: Let justice and righteousness prevail
Names: Nienhuis, Anna, 1984- editor.
Identifiers: Canadiana 20210124490 | ISBN 9781777115548 (softcover)
Subjects: LCSH: Abortion—Sermons. | LCSH: Pro-life movement—Sermons. | LCSH: Abortion—Religious aspects—Christianity. | LCSH: Pro-life movement—Religious aspects—Christianity. | LCSH:
  Christianity—Prayers and devotions.
Classification: LCC HQ767.25 .L48 2021 | DDC 241/.6976—dc23

Published by Reformed Perspective Press
Box 1039 Carman, MB R0G 0J0
www.press.reformedperspective.ca

All Scripture quotations, unless otherwise noted, are from the ESV® Bible (The Holy Bible, English Standard Version®), copyright © 2001 by Crossway, a publishing ministry of Good News Publishers. Used by permission. All rights reserved.

Scripture quotations marked (NIV) are taken from the Holy Bible, New International Version®, NIV®. Copyright © 1973, 1978, 1984, 2011 by Biblica, Inc.® Used by permission of Zondervan. All rights reserved worldwide. www.zondervan.com The "NIV" and "New International Version" are trademarks registered in the United States Patent and Trademark Office by Biblica, Inc.®

Scripture quotations marked (KJV) are taken from the The Authorized (King James) Version. Rights in the Authorized Version in the United Kingdom are vested in the Crown. Reproduced by permission of the Crown's patentee, Cambridge University Press.

CONTENTS

CONTRIBUTORS 9
ACKNOWLEDGEMENTS 14
FOREWORD
    Let justice & righteousness prevail 17
    (A. Schutten)
SERMONS & REFLECTIONS
    Suffering, selfishness, and sacrifice 25
    (W. Bosch)
    Standing in God's armor 35
    (T. VanSpronsen)
    The Lord hates hands that shed innocent blood 43
    (S. Swets)
    Heralds of hope 55
    (J. VanSpronsen)
    Salt & light 63
    (B. Jolliffe)
    A God of choice 77
    (J. Vander Horst)
    How long, O Lord? Wrestling, worshipping, and waiting in
    prayer 89
    (M. Kingswood)
    My eyes shed streams of tears 103
    (G. van Popta)
    What makes people special? 113
    (B. Schoof)
    Facing adversity with courage 123
    (A. C. Pol)

Love the little with big love 133
(B. DeJong)
God uses the weak 145
(D. Lipsy)
Jesus brings life in the midst of death 155
(P. H. Holtvlüwer)
Where there is no vision, the people perish 165
(G. van Popta)
Speak for those who cannot speak for themselves 173
(J. van Popta)
Life is precious 181
(J. Roke)
Pro-life heroines: Shiphrah and Puah 191
(G. van Popta)
Seek justice and righteousness 201
(J. van Popta)
Both hearers and doers 213
(M. Jagt)
Foundational issues 223
(M. Jagt)

EPILOGUE

William Wilberforce: A model of determination 231
(T. Challies)

APPENDIX

Prayers 237

*"What wings are to a bird,
and sails to a ship,
so is prayer to the soul."*

CORRIE TEN BOOM

"Now to him who is able to do immeasurably more than all we ask or imagine, according to his power that is at work within us, to him be glory in the church and in Christ Jesus throughout all generations, for ever and ever!"

EPHESIANS 3:20-21 (NIV)

CONTRIBUTORS

WINSTON BOSCH is married to Berber and is the father of three children – two biological, one adopted, and one more whom the Lord took to himself through miscarriage. He pastors Jubilee Canadian Reformed Church in the nation's capital, was part of a team that started a Safe Families chapter in Ottawa, and has previously served as a missionary in Québec and in Mali, West Africa.

TIM CHALLIES is a Christian, a husband to Aileen, and father to three children. He is a co-founder of Cruciform Press and has written several books, including *The Discipline of Spiritual Discernment* and *Devoted: Great Men and Their Godly Moms*. He worships and serves as a pastor at Grace Fellowship Church in Toronto, ON, and writes daily at www.challies.com.

BILL DEJONG has been a pastor for nearly 25 years in both the US and Canada. Dr. DeJong currently serves at Blessings Christian Church in Hamilton, ON. He is presently chair of the Scripture and Church Seminar of the Tyndale House Scripture Collective (Cambridge, UK) and part-time faculty at Redeemer University in Ancaster, ON. He and his wife Kim, a social worker, have four sons.

PETER H. HOLTVLÜWER has been in full-time gospel ministry since 1999 and currently pastors Ancaster Canadian Reformed Church. He is a co-editor of Clarion magazine and has both edited and contributed to *Christ's Psalms, Our Psalms – Study Resource* (2020) and its companion work the Devotional (2018). He and his wife Erica have received six children.

MARC JAGT grew up in Ontario in a loving Christian home. He was educated at John Calvin School, Guido de Brès High School, McMaster University, and the Canadian Reformed Theological Seminary. He entered the ministry in 1999 and has since pastored Canadian Reformed Churches in Ottawa, ON, Taber, AB and currently Fergus, ON. He is married to his best friend Jody, and they have been blessed with three children.

BEN JOLLIFFE is a pastor, church planter, husband and father in Ottawa, ON. With his wife Jen and two good friends, they planted Resurrection Church in early 2014 and Ben continues as the pastor there. He is a father to Sara, Luke, Ian, and Jake, four fun and rambunctious kids.

MATT KINGSWOOD is the pastor of the Russell Reformed Presbyterian Church in Russell, ON, where he has served since 1997. He is married to Tara and they have six children, and one grandchild (for now!) Matt studied Classics at Carleton University (B.A.) in Ottawa. He then received his theological training at Ottawa Theological Hall and Knox Theological Seminary in Fort Lauderdale, Florida (M.Div.).

DAVID LIPSY and his wife Ruth have been married for 39 years and are blessed with eight children and 24 grandchildren. After attending Rutgers College of Pharmacy for four years, Pastor Lipsy completed a B.A. in Education and served for 14 years as a Christian school teacher and principal in Wisconsin. He received an M.Div. from PRTS in Grand Rapids, MI, completed certificate programs in Biblical Counseling at CCEF in Glenside, PA, and is presently completing the Doctor of Ministry program in counseling from Westminster Seminary in Philadelphia. He has served as pastor for the HRC congregation in New Jersey, Grace Reformed Christian Church in Harrison, AR, and is currently the pastor of the HRC congregation in Burgessville, ON.

ABEL C. POL has been pastoring the Free Reformed Church of Mundijong, Australia since December 2018. His previous charge was the Chilliwack Canadian Reformed Church in British Columbia, where he served for six years after obtaining his M.Div. at the Canadian Reformed Theological Seminary in Hamilton, ON. Rev. Pol and his wife Rosemarie have two children, Caleb and Joash.

JOHN ROKE attended seminary in both the Netherlands and the United States before serving for many years as a Minister of the Word in the Christian Reformed Church. In 1997, he left the Christian Reformed Church and became a Minister of the Word in the United Reformed Church of North America (URCNA). Now an emeritus pastor of the URCNA, he was pastor of Bethel URC in Brockville, ON when he preached the sermon printed in this book. He and his wife Jody currently attend and assist at the Smith Falls Reformed Church, which is affiliated with the Free Church of Scotland.

BEN SCHOOF has been the pastor of Maranatha Canadian Reformed Church in Surrey, BC since 2013. Prior to that he graduated with an M.Div. from the Canadian Reformed Theological Seminary in Hamilton, ON, despite hailing from Perth, Western Australia. He and his wife Danika enjoy spending time in the mountains of the Lower Mainland of BC, along with their four sons, Daniel, Ethan, Leroy & Judah.

STEVEN SWETS is the pastor of Rehoboth United Reformed Church in Hamilton, ON, where he has pastored since 2016. Prior to that, he was a pastor in Abbotsford, BC for seven years. He received his M.Div. at Mid-America Reformed Seminary. He is a native of the Chicago region, and has advocated for the life of the unborn for many years. He is married to Rachel and they have been blessed with four children.

JASON VANDER HORST currently serves as pastor at Surrey Covenant Reformed Church in British Columbia. He was born into a loving Christian home and catechized as a member of Langley Canadian Reformed Church. After earning a B.Kin. from the University of the Fraser Valley and a B.Ed. from the University of British Columbia, Jason taught at a local high school for four years before leaving teaching to pursue an M.Div. from Westminster Seminary California. He and his wife Ardis have two wonderful sons.

GEORGE VAN POPTA earned a B.A. from Trinity Western University in Langley, BC, and an M.Div. from the Canadian Reformed Theological Seminary in Hamilton, ON. He was ordained to the ministry at Jubilee Church in Ottawa from where he left to serve Canadian Reformed Churches in Taber, AB and Ancaster, ON, before ending up back in Ottawa at Jubilee Church. He retired from full-time ministry in 2016 due to declining health. Today he and his wife Dora live in Hamilton, ON, where George keeps active in teaching (especially refugees from abroad), writing hymns, and visiting with family and friends.

JOHN VAN POPTA is Minister Emeritus of Fellowship Canadian Reformed Church in Burlington, ON. He previously served as pastor in Coaldale, AB and Ottawa, ON. He and his wife Bonita have been married for more than 40 years and continue to enjoy God's gifts and grace, including the blessing of 25 grandchildren. John remains active in church life as Associate Pastor to Fellowship Church. He also directs and produces Tyrannus Hall Podcast, which promotes the development of a missional church model.

JULIUS VANSPRONSEN obtained a B.A. at Trinity Western University in Langley, BC and an M.Div. at the Canadian Reformed Theological Seminary in Hamilton, ON. He has served as pastor in the Smithers Canadian Reformed Church and is presently pastor of the Immanuel Canadian Reformed Church in Edmonton, AB. He also spent eight years in Recife, Brazil, working in cooperation with the Reformed Churches in Brazil as a church planter, giving special attention to training men for the office of spiritual leadership in the churches. He and his wife Karen have been blessed with eight children.

TED VANSPRONSEN is currently the pastor of the Canadian Reformed Church in Yarrow, BC. After many jobs, from construction to office work, he went back to university to get his degree and then completed his seminary studies. After serving in Busselton, West Australia, Ted, his wife Cathy and their two daughters are now enjoying living in the Fraser Valley, BC.

ACKNOWLEDGEMENTS

I (Anna) am thankful to André for conceiving the idea for this project, and then trusting it in my hands. As a faithful witness in the public square, he leads by example and encourages others to get involved alongside him. He saw a need for prayer services and then did the work to bring them to life, resulting in earnest, communal prayer to end abortion and the Scripture-rooted sermons and reflections we were able to compile here.

I (André) am thankful to have been able to work on this project with the general editor of the collection, Anna Nienhuis. God has gifted her to be a master of words. Her edits to these sermons (originally meant to be presented orally) make them a delight to read as well. Many preachers don't type their sermons word for word – often Anna took point-form notes and converted them into readable prose. Her helpful prayer points and thought-provoking study questions make this a versatile book for group study or personal or family devotions.

Together, we thank Jubilee Church and her members for faithfully hosting and then co-sponsoring the March for Life prayer service in Ottawa for 15 years now. From the beginning, you provided the volunteers to ensure those who marched did so while physically fed and nourished. While man does not live on bread alone, a sandwich sure helps fight the fight!

Over the past 15 years, 18 Reformed or Presbyterian pastors from six different denominations were willing to bring the Word of God to Christians before they walked in the March for Life. Thank you, pastors, for preaching passionately on this pressing moral issue, and for now sharing what you preached in this collection so that many more can benefit from these calls to courage and compassion, to prayer and action. May God hear and answer the prayers lifted in response to reading your words herein.

Thanks to Chelsea Huebert from Third Floor Design Studio for the beautiful cover design, and to RP Press and the staff there for assisting with the publishing and distribution of this volume.

Thank you also to our detail-oriented friends who generously gave their time to do a thorough copy edit on this book — Andrea De Haan, Andrew Vanderveen and Lisa Van Dam.

A heartfelt thank you also goes to our ARPA colleagues, who encouraged us to see this project through and who march with us every day. These colleagues are also friends, and brothers and sisters in the faith, and it is a joy and delight to work and walk alongside each of them in the striving for justice.

Above all, thanks go to God, for being the perfect picture of justice, righteousness, mercy and grace, the One whose Spirit moves Christians to a living and active faith. We are thankful that He has made it possible that we could reflect on the growth of prayer services, the increased volume and courage of Christian voices in the public square, and the knowledge that we are not alone in this fight, but surrounded and preceded by so great a cloud of witnesses. To Him be the glory for ever and ever.

A.N. & A.M.S.

LET JUSTICE AND RIGHTEOUSNESS PREVAIL

Foreword

BY ANDRÉ SCHUTTEN

"But let justice roll on like a river, righteousness like a never-failing stream." - Amos 5:24

Since 2006, Reformed churches have held prayer services in conjunction with the annual March for Life. These prayer services are meant to encourage and equip Christians in the battle for hearts and minds when it comes to the issue of abortion. The book you hold is a collection of all the sermons and meditations given at these March for Life prayer services from 2006 to 2020. I hope and pray that, through this collection, the Biblical encouragement contained in those services can spread far beyond those who have been able to attend a March for Life prayer service.

Reflecting on the 20 sermons in this collection, I am impressed by the wide variety of texts preached on. Incredibly, even though the focus of every service was on the same topic – abortion – only one text was preached on twice, even though we always invited the preacher to select his own text. This speaks to the broad applicability of Scripture to this moral issue of our time, and the consistent Biblical call to hate and oppose injustice, seek righteousness, and honour life.

Throughout the book of Amos, the prophet rages against the injustices all around him. Amos denounces the material excesses of the Israelites as they turn a blind eye to injustice. Amos 5 and 6 contain some moving poetry that strongly decries religious hypocrisy, materialism, and injustice. God had Amos use very strong language: "I hate, I despise your feasts, and I take no delight in your solemn assemblies." (Amos 5:21). Religious devotion is meaningless if it is accompanied by unfair or oppressive taxes (5:11), oppression of the poor or bribery (5:12), or turning a blind eye and remaining silent and unmoved in the face of injustice (6:1-6).

I imagine that Amos would have a similar word for the Church in Canada today if we turn a blind eye to the greatest injustice of our time: the fully funded and publicly celebrated yearly slaughter of 100,000 of the most innocent among us. The annual March for Life prayer services properly ground and humble us as we face the task of addressing the ongoing evil of abortion and its impact on all Canadians.

MODEST BEGINNINGS

In 2005, my friend Henk Huijgen, my cousin Sarah van Popta, and I helped form McMaster Lifeline, a group of idealistic and enthusiastic pro-life university students. As part of our pro-life activity, we travelled from Hamilton to Ottawa in May of that year to attend our first-ever National March for Life. Since we were travelling with another dozen or so members of our club, all of whom were Roman Catholic, we tagged along with them to the Mass, which they celebrated immediately before gathering on Parliament Hill. Being Protestants, we merely observed, and afterwards agreed that there really ought to be a Protestant prayer service as well. So, the following year, we planned one.

In the lead-up to May of 2006, I contacted Rev. Marc Jagt, the pastor of the Canadian Reformed Church in Ottawa (not yet named Jubilee Church). He agreed to lead a prayer service for us, so we organized a carpool with a couple dozen Protestant McMaster students heading to Ottawa again. Some members of the Ottawa congregation supplied us with water bottles, granola bars, and sandwiches on the day of the march, and the tradition of them providing lunches for March for Life participants was born.

In 2007, we grew from a few dozen to nearly 100 attendees, as I organized two coach buses to head to Ottawa from southern Ontario. We continued to meet in the Merivale United Church building, and after the prayer service we went to downtown Ottawa for the March for Life.

The challenges in those early years included logistics, but there was also some resistance to the very idea of marching for a cause. Should Christians protest? There were some within my own Reformed Christian community who were really uncomfortable with the idea at the time. But we reasoned, discussed, considered, and persisted, and I am so thankful for how the prayer services have grown alongside the rise of Reformed Christian voices in the political arena.

THE PRO-LIFE PRAYER SERVICE MATURES

In the summer of 2011, I began working for ARPA Canada and, in the spring of 2012, as an ARPA employee and as a member of Ottawa's Jubilee Church, I had the privilege of taking a lead role again in organizing the prayer service. We moved the prayer service to First Baptist Church in downtown Ottawa, just a short walk from Parliament Hill, and we've been meeting – and growing – there ever since.

As the years passed, more ARPA staff became involved in helping, and we also began livestreaming the service. The Reformed prayer service grew from less than 40 to more than 400 people, now with standing room only! At most of the prayer services, we took up collections netting thousands of dollars for different organizations including Safe Families, First Place Pregnancy Options, Beginnings Adoption Agency, and the Pregnancy Care Centre in Toronto. The Christian community is not just against abortion; we are also there to support women choosing life!

In the last few years, ARPA Canada also began to assist with regional Marches for Life, helping organize the March in Victoria, British Columbia and Toronto, Ontario. In conjunction with the March, we also began organizing prayer services in these cities, as well as Edmonton, Alberta. Sermons from these regional prayer services have been included in this collection as well.

As the pro-life prayer service matured, there were changes and developments happening in the pro-life movement as well. Politically, a sense of hopelessness and disengagement changed to prayerful, active hopefulness. We saw many more Christians get involved and become passionate about the cause, and, most encouraging of all, young people dominated the scene. The pro-life movement was (and is!) energetic, strategic, and growing, with Christians at the forefront.

WE WILL NOT BE SATISFIED UNTIL...

In 1969, Prime Minister Pierre Elliot Trudeau passed an omnibus criminal law amendment which, among other things, legalized abortion in limited circumstances. That law was passed on the second Thursday of May, and so the March for Life is always held on the second Thursday of May.

The Canadian Charter of Rights and Freedoms, added to our Constitution – the highest law of the land – in 1982, was to guarantee the inalienable rights of life, liberty, and security of the person (in section 7). It is obvious today that Canada has defaulted on this promise insofar as pre-born children are concerned. Instead of honouring this sacred obligation, the Supreme Court of Canada used that very section of the Charter to strike down the 1969 abortion law on January 28, 1988 in the infamous Morgentaler case, leaving us with no legal restriction on abortion whatsoever. The following year, in a case called Borowski, the Court refused outright to hear arguments for why the protection of section 7 of the Charter should apply to pre-born children. And, though the Court left it open to Parliament to create a new law, to this day Parliament has refused to rectify this injustice. There is no legal protection at all for any pre-born child in Canada up until birth. There is no justice in Canada for any pre-born child whose life is intentionally snuffed out. As long as this injustice prevails, we will not be satisfied.

Martin Luther King Jr. was a man well acquainted with injustice. Racism was the preeminent moral issue of his day, and injustice and hypocrisy were rampant. In his famous 1963 "I Have a Dream" speech in Washington, DC, King cited the words from Amos 5 quoted above. When he was asked when "the negro" would be satisfied, King passionately declared, "We will not be satisfied until 'justice rolls down like waters and righteousness like a mighty stream.'" That ought to be our rally-cry as well: may we not be satisfied while injustice prevails. May the prayer services, the sermons, the marches, the lobbying, the litigation, and the protests continue until justice rolls down like waters and righteousness like a mighty stream.

King urged his followers, "We must forever conduct our struggle on the high plane of dignity and discipline. We must not allow our creative protest to degenerate into physical violence."

TO CHANNEL KING FURTHER...

As we walk, we must make the pledge that we shall always march ahead. We cannot turn back. There are those who are asking the devotees of civil rights, "When will you be satisfied?" We can never be satisfied as long as the pre-born child is the victim of the unspeakable horrors of abortion. We can never be satisfied as long as their bodies are torn apart and discarded as medical waste. We can never be satisfied as long as Canadian children are stripped of their personhood and robbed of their dignity by the language of "choice." We cannot be satisfied as long as a seven-month-old pre-born child can be murdered together with her mother, and the law counts only one victim. We can never be satisfied when a baby girl can be destroyed simply because she's a girl. We can never be satisfied when the mother of a baby boy diagnosed with Down syndrome is urged repeatedly by her doctor to kill the child. We can never be satisfied as long as laws fund abortion but won't fund abortion alternatives, and laws prohibit offering help outside an abortion mill but let the abortionists make their advertisements and profits. No, no, we are not satisfied, and we will not be satisfied until justice rolls down like waters, and righteousness like a mighty stream.

The hundreds of thousands who marched with King had come a very long way, spanning centuries. King urged them then not to "wallow in the valley of despair." He used Scripture to encourage those fighting for the full and equal protection of the law. He said:

> I have a dream that one day every valley shall be exalted, every hill and mountain shall be made low, the rough places will be made plain, and the crooked places will be made straight, and the glory of the Lord shall be revealed, and all flesh shall see it together.
>
> ...With this faith we will be able to hew out of the mountain of despair a stone of hope. With this faith we will be able to transform the jangling discords of our nation into a beautiful symphony of brotherhood. With this faith we will be able to work together, to pray together, to struggle together, to go to jail together, to stand up for freedom together, knowing that we will be free one day.

So too, when facing massive opposition or total apathy in our legislatures, courts, and culture, when facing the horror and injustice and entrenchment of abortion, nevertheless, with this faith we will persist. We will work together, pray together, struggle together, even go to jail together, to stand up for the protection of life for the most vulnerable, knowing that one day there will be justice and righteousness.

My hope is that, as the Christian community continues to work, we always also continue to pray. May this collection of prayer service meditations and messages be a useful tool for you as you pray to end abortion in Canada; may it encourage you to keep up the good fight, and point you to the source of Life and Light, the God from whom justice rolls down like waters, and righteousness like a mighty stream.

1 KINGS 3:16-28

Then two prostitutes came to the king and stood before him. The one woman said, "Oh, my lord, this woman and I live in the same house, and I gave birth to a child while she was in the house. Then on the third day after I gave birth, this woman also gave birth. And we were alone. There was no one else with us in the house; only we two were in the house. And this woman's son died in the night, because she lay on him. And she arose at midnight and took my son from beside me, while your servant slept, and laid him at her breast, and laid her dead son at my breast. When I rose in the morning to nurse my child, behold, he was dead. But when I looked at him closely in the morning, behold, he was not the child that I had borne." But the other woman said, "No, the living child is mine, and the dead child is yours." The first said, "No, the dead child is yours, and the living child is mine." Thus they spoke before the king.

Then the king said, "The one says, 'This is my son that is alive, and your son is dead'; and the other says, 'No; but your son is dead, and my son is the living one.'" And the king said, "Bring me a sword." So a sword was brought before the king. And the king said, "Divide the living child in two, and give half to the one and half to the other." Then the woman whose son was alive said to the king, because her heart yearned for her son, "Oh, my lord, give her the living child, and by no means put him to death." But the other said, "He shall be neither mine nor yours; divide him."

Then the king answered and said, "Give the living child to the first woman, and by no means put him to death; she is his mother." And all Israel heard of the judgment that the king had rendered, and they stood in awe of the king, because they perceived that the wisdom of God was in him to do justice.

SUFFERING, SELFISHNESS, AND SACRIFICE

WINSTON BOSCH
Ottawa, 2020

Suggested song: **PSALM 20**
Scripture reading: 1 **KINGS 3:16-28**

As we consider the topic of abortion, my mind goes to the prayer of Solomon in 1 Kings 3. In this chapter, the Lord God asks Solomon what he would like the Lord to give him and Solomon prays this prayer: "Give your servant an understanding mind to govern your people, that I may discern between good and evil."

That's a beautiful prayer, and isn't that also a prayer we should pray for our own government? Our sincere prayer should be that God would give our government an understanding mind to govern the people of this land; that the Lord would give the government discernment between good and evil, also in terms of life and death, of life and abortion.

The author of 1 Kings 3 notes this prayer of Solomon, and then goes through the legal records of his day and finds evidence of how the Lord answered Solomon's prayer. That legal courtroom transcript is found in 1 Kings 3:16-28. This example is undoubtedly one of many that could have been chosen, and it vividly illustrates how the Lord gave Solomon the gift of great wisdom, an understanding mind to govern, and discernment between good and evil, right and wrong.

This is a passage of Scripture that the author has recorded under the inspiration of the Holy Spirit. What I'd like to do is take this story and use it as a springboard for prayer to help us pray concerning abortion in the country of Canada.

SUFFERING AND SELFISHNESS

The first thing that I would like to note from this story is the existence of both suffering and selfishness. The passage starts, "Then two prostitutes came." When you hear the word "prostitute," the first thing that should come to your mind is suffering.

Prostitution is violence against women. Prostitution is intrinsically exploitative and anti-women. Research has shown that 90% of women involved in prostitution would like to escape it, but can't figure out a way to do so and still survive. So, when we read "two prostitutes" we ought to think of suffering. These women suffer at the hands of men, and here they both become pregnant – and the fathers are, of course, nowhere to be seen. They're pregnant and alone.

I think that suffering is a good place to start as we think about what to pray when we pray that abortion might end in Canada. It helps us to think of the suffering that many women undergo at the hands of men. Many women are impregnated by men who do not want to take responsibility for children. Some women are pressured into abortions, or abused or abandoned by men. There is so much suffering behind abortion. Women feel like they have no choice, no other option, like they're being forced down a road that ends at an abortion clinic.

Once there, women are suffering at the hands of a big abortion industry that is, at its very heart, anti-women. The abortion industry tells women that being a mom is a weakness, and that killing your baby is a strength. It is an industry that profits off of suffering. Abortion doesn't help women out of the surrounding problems of their life. Abortion doesn't help women to leave abuse. Abortion doesn't help women with the financial insecurity they experience or their general feeling of being unsupported. What abortion does is get men off the hook while making women suffer the physical, the mental, and the emotional scars that abortion often leaves in its wake.

As we pray, we who are pro-life must remember and pray for women who are suffering. Women who feel trapped. Women who feel like they have nowhere to go, that they're pressured on all sides, that they've been abandoned by men, who can see no way forward with a baby. Women who are suffering and about to abort their baby.

But as we read this story, we move quickly from suffering to selfishness. This selfishness is represented in the story of the second woman. She awakes in the night and finds that she has accidentally smothered her baby. She takes the limp, dead child, sneaks into her housemate's room, and exchanges her dead baby for the live baby. While there is certainly sadness and suffering here, it results in a horrific sin of selfishness: a cruel act of kidnapping, a lie, the stealing of the joy of motherhood from another and giving the devastation of infant death. Then the horror of her selfishness takes on a new depth when she is confronted by the king. The selfish act that she committed against another woman now becomes a selfish murderous act committed against a baby.

You can see the scene: the soldier holds the living baby, brandishing a sword as the wise king seeks to discern between good and evil, and evil shows its face. Selfishness shows its face. And in its ugliness, it hisses from the lips of the second woman, "He shall be neither mine nor yours. Divide him! Cut him in two!"

This is where the sin of selfishness leads us, doesn't it? It leads us also today to men and women so consumed by their own agenda, men and women so consumed by their own plans, men and women so insistent that nothing will defy their will, that nothing will stand between them and their desires, their wants, their plans, their comfort, their convenience, that they're willing to say, "This living baby shall be neither mine nor yours. Cut him in two." It's a horrific and a realistic picture of the selfish horror inherent in abortion. "My plans come first. My life comes first. My desires must be first. Cut him in two. Rip her apart with a vacuum suction device. Use a clamp to dismember him, cut her into pieces. Remove this child from my womb, for this baby shall be neither mine nor yours."

We rightly shed compassionate tears and say compassionate prayers for the many women who are suffering as a result of abortion and its impacts. But we must also be willing to speak truth and to pray truth against the selfishness of men and women who leave a wake of dead babies behind them. "He shall be neither mine nor yours. Cut him in two." Pray for the suffering, and for the selfish, that they might see a Saviour and turn to Him.

SACRIFICE

This text speaks of suffering and selfishness, and we see those all around us – and inside of ourselves – in the world in which we live. But now we move from suffering and selfishness to sacrifice. We see this in verse 26: "Then the woman whose son was alive said to the king, because her heart yearned for her son, 'O my lord, give her the living child and by no means put him to death!'"

This prostitute whose child was alive, this woman's heart understood that love and life are bound tightly together. This woman knew that children ought to be yearned for and protected. This woman teaches us something about the sanctity of life and about the sacrifices to be made to keep babies alive. "Give this living child to another woman! Don't allow this child to die." From this prostitute, this suffering woman, we hear no selfish talk come from her mouth. There's no reasoning that, "Well, this child can live if it suits me. The child can live, but on my conditions." There's none of this talk that, "The child can live if I can provide them a good home," or "The child can live only if I can be the mother that I want to be." Instead, selfishness is replaced by sacrifice. "Lord, King, give the child to another woman if it will save a life. Give my child to my lying brothel roommate. Let her adopt him, only let the child live!" Only let the child live. This woman is willing to sacrifice her right of motherhood, her right of parenthood, if only the child can live. This is love for life.

Pray that the Lord would teach us sacrifice, that we would want to learn from the good prostitute. There's so much suffering in this world. There's so much sin and selfishness in this world. But when it comes to the sanctity of life, when it comes to the life of little unborn children, it's sacrifice that must win over sin and suffering. Is that not the Jesus way? That is the example that our Lord Jesus Christ set for us at great cost – suffering is won over and sin is beaten by sacrifice. So, as believers who treasure the sanctity of God-created life, it's important for us to realize that when we speak about the sanctity of life, sacrifice is needed to overcome the suffering and sin that lead to abortion.

It's easy to say that it's the pregnant moms, the distressed dating couples, or the overwhelmed parents who don't want another child must sacrifice their selfish dreams in order to save a child. And that's true, of course. But it's also you and me, we who live in the shadow of the cross of Jesus, who must be ready to sacrifice. We must be ready to sacrifice our time, and our money, and our reputations, and our plans, and our comfort for the sake of the unborn. The sin of abortion must be met by the church's willingness to sacrifice. The suffering and the sin of abortion must be met by the sacrifice of adoption and fostering, and homes and churches that provide safe places for pregnant women to have their children. Our cry must be, "Lord, I'm willing to take up my cross and I'm willing to open my home and I'm willing to extend my table if only you let the children live! If only the child will live."

GOVERNANCE AND GOD

This gripping story in 1 Kings 3 ends beautifully with these words in verse 27: "Then the King answered and said, 'Give the living child to the first woman and by no means put him to death. She is his mother.'" Solomon recognizes that the essence of motherhood is unselfish, sacrificial love. In awarding the baby to the woman willing to sacrifice her interest for the baby's welfare, Solomon embraces the sanctity of life over self.

And so, we pray that we might see in our day an understanding mind and a discernment between good and evil in our government. And we can pray for the same wisdom and discernment for ourselves. We have seen that this is a prayer that the Lord delights to answer.

We pray that our government would be willing to help the suffering, but not indulge the selfish. We pray that our government would recognize the sanctity of life and not support the termination of life. We pray that they would support and encourage sacrifice, not sin.

In 1 Kings 3 we have a court record, a legal record concerning a child in danger, a child whom one woman is willing to have cut in two. The court record ends with the king's wise ruling, "By no means put him to death!" That is what we pray for when we pray to end abortion – that we would hear those words from our government: "By no means put the unborn to death!" We pray that we might one day hear and have written before us a legal record, an official proclamation of Parliament stating, "We recognize the pre-born child as a human being and we have amended the Criminal Code to say abortion is illegal. By no means put the children to death!" That is our prayer, a prayer for God to move in a way that only He can.

Until the Lord answers our prayer as He answered Solomon's prayer, we continue to give our lives as living sacrifices so that, in this world of suffering and selfishness, the sanctity of life might not be ignored. Because this, brothers and sisters, is the Jesus way.

It was Jesus who, in Matthew 12, said that He was greater than Solomon. The great Messianic King came to earth as an unborn child in His mother's womb. Jesus, who came to this earth to suffer. Jesus, who loved and befriended and ate meals with and taught prostitutes as His own disciples. Jesus, who denounced selfishness with His sacrificial love on the cross. Jesus, who maintained the sanctity of life against murder and yet willingly gave Himself up to be murdered, nailed to a cross. Jesus, who rose again to sit on the throne as the greater Solomon, where He sits today, that we might all be in awe of the King, perceiving in Him the wisdom of God to do justice. Jesus, who knows the plight of every aborted child. Jesus, who will judge with justice. Jesus, who governs from heaven today with goodness and grace. Jesus, who one day will return to demonstrate conclusively that, through sacrifice, sin and suffering will be no more. Jesus, who one day will issue the order, "By no means put those children to death." Our Lord Jesus Christ is our guarantee that one day all abortion will come to an end.

PRAYER POINTS

- Pray for those who are suffering and feeling trapped in difficult circumstances, especially women facing an unplanned and unwanted pregnancy
- Thank God for His example of great sacrifice, and pray for His strength to live a sacrificial life in His service
- Pray for the blessing of courage to defend and support life
- Pray that God would give you words to speak with grace and truth, that others would be called to true repentance from selfishness and so bring glory to God

DISCUSSION QUESTIONS

1. Read 1 Peter 2, and consider verse 21 in this context. To what have we been called, and how does that impact how we use our voice in the public square?

2. The theme of sacrifice runs throughout Scripture. Meditate on what Christ was willing to sacrifice in order to save us from our condemnation. Think of other biblical examples where selfishness was overcome by sacrifice.

3. Consider everything we are asked to be willing to sacrifice in order to let the children live – home, time, privacy, money, reputation, comfort, etc. Which of these are you most resistant to sacrificing when you consider how you could be involved in pro-life action?

4. Many today are focused on self, and what they get out of their relationships. How has this attitude impacted us as Christians in relationships? How can you practice love that puts sacrifice before selfishness in your own life, for example as a friend, co-worker, client, sibling, parent, or spouse?

EPHESIANS 6:10-20

Finally, be strong in the Lord and in the strength of his might. Put on the whole armor of God, that you may be able to stand against the schemes of the devil. For we do not wrestle against flesh and blood, but against the rulers, against the authorities, against the cosmic powers over this present darkness, against the spiritual forces of evil in the heavenly places.

Therefore take up the whole armor of God, that you may be able to withstand in the evil day, and having done all, to stand firm. Stand therefore, having fastened on the belt of truth, and having put on the breastplate of righteousness, and, as shoes for your feet, having put on the readiness given by the gospel of peace. In all circumstances take up the shield of faith, with which you can extinguish all the flaming darts of the evil one; and take the helmet of salvation, and the sword of the Spirit, which is the Word of God, praying at all times in the Spirit, with all prayer and supplication.

To that end, keep alert with all perseverance, making supplication for all the saints, and also for me, that words may be given to me in opening my mouth boldly to proclaim the mystery of the gospel, for which I am an ambassador in chains, that I may declare it boldly, as I ought to speak.

STANDING IN GOD'S ARMOR

TED VANSPRONSEN
Victoria, 2019

Suggested song: **A MIGHTY FORTRESS IS OUR GOD**
Scripture reading: **EPHESIANS 6:10-20**

To my fellow warriors in our Lord Jesus Christ.

Yes, warriors! What we just read sure sounds like a soldier preparing himself for battle, doesn't it? Be strong in the Lord, in His mighty power! That is the encouraging Word of God we find in Ephesians 6. Be strengthened by God's power, and in that power, stand. Stand against the schemes and cunning ways of our greatest enemy: the devil and his spiritual forces.

THE BRIEFING

The fact of the matter is, if you are a Christian, a follower of Christ Jesus, then your life cannot be lived without a spiritual battle. We are all involved in a battle, in war.

Now, as with any battle or fight, it is important that we know our enemy. Thankfully, God's Word does not leave us in the dark when it comes to this. We read in Ephesians 6 how the devil is cunning, scheming, and we are called to stand against his wily ways. We are also clearly told that, though he may use people as his agents, we do not ultimately wrestle against "flesh and blood," but against the "powers of this dark world," and against the "spiritual forces of evil in the heavenly realms." We are at war! Consider this message as your military briefing before you go out. God's Word clearly tells us an "unseen world" exists. And we are called to stand our ground against dark spiritual forces.

For us today living in this Western world, the unseen spiritual realm is not something we often think about. We are more focused on science, and growing in knowledge about our physical universe. This can dull our sense of the spiritual. Let us be reminded that "though we live in the world, we do not wage war like the world does," as Paul writes to the Corinthians in 2 Corinthians 10. We do not use the weapons of the world, but we are called to put on the armor of God. God equips us to stand against the schemes of our enemy!

THE ARMOR

Many Christians are quite familiar with this passage of Scripture about the armor of God. I won't go through all the different pieces of equipment we are given, but there are a few things I'd like to bring to your attention.

First of all, it is very clear that being strong in the Lord has everything to do with "standing." Four times in four verses we are called to stand firm in our faith. It is interesting that the Holy Spirit does not suggest we head out on the offensive. Rather, we stand with the shield of faith so that we might extinguish the fiery darts of the evil one. As John Bunyan pointed out, we are not given armor for our backs. No, we stand ready to face the enemy head on!

Among the armor we are given we find only two offensive weapons, and only one, the sword (or dagger) suggests actual fighting. The weapons we are given in this spiritual fight are the "sword of the Spirit," that is the Word of God, and prayer. There aren't many weapons, but the ones we have are incredibly powerful. We see then that being called to "stand" does not mean we are to be inactive. We are to be busy with the Word and with prayer. A passive Christian is an oxymoron! There is a real battle going on, and we are either for God or against Him. Believers are given God's Word and access to God in prayer, and called to use both.

If we are looking for an example to follow, there is none better than Jesus Himself. In Isaiah 59:17, we learn that Jesus puts on the armor of God, the same armor we are given! Jesus puts on the armor and fights for justice, fights for us. In the New Testament, three times Jesus used the "sword of the spirit" against the tempter (see Matthew 4). For every temptation Satan presented in the desert, Jesus answered with Scripture. Jesus was fully equipped, expecting and prepared for battle.

And so, let us also regularly equip and strengthen ourselves as we grow in our knowledge and understanding, not of the world, but of the Word. Only then will we be properly equipped for a battle that is not of this world. Only then will we be filled with the same power and readiness that Jesus had, to defend ourselves against the onslaught of the enemy.

PRAY IN THE SPIRIT

In all this, my fellow soldiers, we pray. We clothe ourselves with each piece of armor, and we pray. We must continue in prayer, for we simply cannot engage the enemy without praying to our God – He calls us to be strong in the Lord, and He is the only source of that strength. The command to "be strong in the Lord" can be translated literally as "be strengthened." In other words, we don't strengthen ourselves; we are to be constantly empowered by God!

Notice that we are told to pray "in the Spirit." The Spirit of Jesus was sent to live in our hearts. Our whole lives are lived "in the Spirit." Just as God gives us armor to protect us against the evil one, so He gives the Spirit to help us pray, and because He lives in us we can be assured that our prayers will be heard, and He will give us the power to stand (see Romans 8:26).

When we live our lives not only in the Spirit, but also in Jesus Christ, we never have to worry that we won't be given His power. And what mighty power this is – it is the same power that was able to raise Jesus from the dead! Apart from Christ we can do nothing. But through God's power, we can be strong in the Lord. Thank God that we have available to us all the strength of His might!

A SPIRITUAL BATTLE

Brothers and sisters, our enemy Satan and the powers of darkness are very busy in our world today – and we are called to stand against them. It can sometimes seem that "our ancient foe" is almost getting the upper hand today. People seem to care more for the rights of animals than the unborn, truth is determined by how people perceive it to be, and even our gender is left to how we feel about ourselves.

Oh, what schemes our enemy uses! That is why we simply must understand that our battle is not against people, but against spiritual forces of evil. Oh sure, he uses human instruments – but the real battle is spiritual. And so, be strong in the Lord, my fellow soldiers. Know we are given mighty power. Let's daily put on the armor of God and live with the sword of the Spirit in our hands.

And, let's keep praying! Not only is our posture one of standing in battle formation, we also "stand" by getting down on our knees. That is how we will be empowered by God's mighty power.

One thing we can be sure of: we need not fear, for God has "willed His truth to triumph through us." By way of the cross, Jesus Christ has disarmed and triumphed over the powers of the evil one. When we are united by faith to the victorious Christ, and make use of the armor He gives us, we truly can be strong in the Lord.

Amen, so shall it be!

PRAYER POINTS

- Thank God for His Word, which equips us to stand against the devil
- Ask God for wisdom, that you may lean on His strength rather than your own, and bring to mind Scripture to repel Satan's attacks
- Pray for courage to stand, to face evil in God's strength

- Pray for the ability to show love to people who disagree with you or disobey God's Word, recognizing that our struggle is ultimately against the powers of darkness
- Thank God that victory has been won, that we can be confident that the truth will triumph

DISCUSSION QUESTIONS

1. Read Isaiah 59:14-17. How does it encourage you to know that Jesus put on the armor of God?

2. How can we increase our awareness of the spiritual realm and the invisible battle going on around us? Are you able to see bad things in our culture as part of this greater darkness, or do you tend to criticize individuals and specific sins? How do you also see God's hand in these things, and remain confident that He has won the victory?

3. Look up Matthew 4:1-11. Consider how Satan's lies had pieces of truth, and see how Jesus refutes his lies with Scripture. What are some half-truths that tempt Christians today?

4. Consider the comfort of "living your whole life in the Spirit." How can this encourage us when we aren't sure what or how to pray?

PROVERBS 6:16-19

There are six things that the Lord hates,
seven that are an abomination to him:
haughty eyes, a lying tongue,
and hands that shed innocent blood,
a heart that devises wicked plans,
feet that make haste to run to evil,
a false witness who breathes out lies,
and one who sows discord among brothers.

THE LORD HATES HANDS THAT SHED INNOCENT BLOOD

STEVEN SWETS
Toronto, 2019

Suggested song: **PSALM 133**
Scripture reading: **PROVERBS 6:16-19**

There are many emotions and many angles at which to come at a subject like abortion. There are many moving parts, people, and policies. There are voiceless victims, guilt-ridden mothers, and confused fathers. But no matter how one is impacted by abortion, know for sure that it impacts each of us. It impacts the fabric of this great nation; it impacts the present and the future. We live in a country where an ultrasound can be a death sentence for a little Canadian girl whose parents wanted a boy, where a genetic difference like Down Syndrome can be cause for death. Sacrificed on the altar of convenience, ambition, an independent lifestyle, are our nation's children. Let's pause together to see what God calls us to as responsible citizens of a nation.

Proverbs 6:16-17 says that "The LORD hates...hands that shed innocent blood." This is a biblical principle, and passages like Genesis 9:6, Exodus 20:13 and Deut. 27:25a all make a similar point. The shedding of innocent blood is unjust, and therefore is hated by a just God. There are four points I want to briefly draw out of this biblical principle.

OPEN YOUR EYES

In the parable of the Good Samaritan in Luke 10, there were seemingly righteous men who turned a blind eye to the plight of a man half-dead on the side of the path. They knew he was there, but they had excuses. Excuses are not hard to come by. After all, we too can see people in need and be quick to think, well, that is none of my business. We might say sorry, I don't have time, I have an important meeting or some place to be. In the parable, the Levite might have thought, I am a minister, I cannot become unclean before the Lord. But that wasn't love, and love is the greatest of Christian virtues, the "fulfillment of the law" (Romans 13:10).

The fact of the matter is that thousands of helpless pre-born children die each year in Canada due to abortion. These are thousands of lives ended which could – and should – be preserved. That this is happening isn't a secret; in fact, it is sometimes even celebrated in this country! Turning a blind eye to this tragedy does not honour God. We must be aware and do what we can to make others aware. Live with your eyes wide open. After all, these are our neighbours we are talking about here, neighbours we are called to love as we love ourselves. Let us never turn a blind eye to the plight of innocents.

THINK OF YOUR COUNTRY

The primary purpose of civil government is to ensure that justice and peace reign in the land and that the lives, property and freedom of its citizens are properly defended (Psalm 72). No country can be blessed by God when it does not protect its citizens. God gave the civil government the power of the sword to protect, not to harm. Romans 13 is a New Testament outworking of Genesis 9:6 which says, "Whoever sheds the blood of man, by man shall his blood be shed, for God made man in his own image." This is the role of the government in punishing evildoers.

But listen to the very next verse from Genesis 9: "And you, be fruitful and multiply; increase greatly on the earth and multiply in it." Obviously, this is the blessing of new life, the opposite of ending life! Ending the life of man is to be sanctioned only by the government, and only when he or she has taken the life of another. New life is always to be celebrated and protected.

When the question of abortion comes up, it is often a question of convenience. Maybe it is an unexpected pregnancy or some other crisis, but the focus often stops there, instead of on the options available. We fail to look for better, if harder, solutions because abortion is seen as a relatively easy fix.

The picture of a bullying boyfriend or husband who pressures his wife or girlfriend into having an abortion is true sometimes, but not always. The mantra that it is the woman's body and she can do with it what she wants has also hurt many fathers. Many men feel no sense of responsibility because our culture has told him that pregnancy is a woman's problem, and not his responsibility. We have a nation of grieving mothers, and also grieving or absent fathers.

Our nation should not be providing abortion, a sinful "easy way out" that is far from easy for many post-abortive women. We should point people to options and the church should be involved in this as well, offering support. Let us emphasize the options, including fostering children and adoption.

HATE WHAT THE LORD HATES

We read that the Lord hates the hand that sheds innocent blood. Yes, the government has the role to punish wickedness. However, when the government is not doing that, which is the case right now, the citizens must petition the government. People might enter politics for a number of different reasons, but we need to let them know what their responsibility is as leaders in our nation. When someone becomes part of the legislature, it is easy for all their time to be consumed in their work, not pausing to think about their role in the broader context.

What makes our petitions more urgent, and morally obligatory, is the fact that our government has sanctioned legal death. Not having any abortion laws is no better than having wicked abortion laws. Injustice is being done to those who have no voice, no rights, and no power to object. The government sanctions legalized murder.

There are too many examples in the last century of governments sanctioning the murder of their own citizens. Whether it was the Armenian genocide around 1915 when 1.5 million Armenians were horrifically killed by Turkish government troops, or Stalin's starving of millions of Ukrainians by giving them grain quotas that were impossible to fill, or the Nazi genocide of Jews and gypsies, or the

Rwandan genocide, or Canadians murdering their own children year after year, is there a difference? Which of those is the worst? The one that happens in a clinic, behind closed doors, with quality medical care and no screams to be heard, may seem a little less horrific. But it is not.

How can we as a nation look back with contempt on other atrocities committed while we have government-sanctioned death squads who wear white gowns and work in a hygienic facility? May God help us.

TAKE ACTION

Since the Lord hates the shedding of innocent blood, we are called to hate it as well, and as a result, we are called to take action.

The first step is to pray. Pray for those in authority over us. Pray for the executive, legislative, and judicial branches of government. Pray that God might raise up courageous men and women who are willing to stand on conviction to defend those who cannot defend themselves. Pray for the changing of minds, but especially pray for the changing and the softening of hearts, a turning to God in repentance and sorrow. We are all sinners, and once a sinner realizes that they are unable to please God by their own might, they must flee to the Saviour, the only one who ever truly, fully loved His neighbour. What greater love is there than a man who lays down his life for his friends?

Let us also work. All across Canada courageous citizens are standing up to speak for those who do not have a voice. If we think of the great civil rights movements in American and Canadian history, we know those movements began with concerned citizens, not with politicians. Let us be those concerned citizens. Continue to stand up for truth and righteousness to reign in our land. Vote pro-life, support groups that work to make it clear that abortion is unacceptable, speak love with your wallets. Support pregnancy care centres in your community, and pray for a change of heart for undecided pregnant women. Be willing to open your home to children from crisis pregnancies, perhaps even through fostering or adoption.

Let us pray and work, all the while knowing that we have a God who sits on the throne, ruling all. Christ is Lord over this nation. As His children and His ambassadors, let us seek freedom for all, at whatever stage of life they might be.

PRAYER POINTS

- Pray for our governments, that they may recognize God's power and turn to Him for wisdom
- Pray for Christian politicians specifically, that they may have courage and conviction and be good ambassadors for Christ
- Pray for revival, for changed hearts and a desire to serve God
- Ask forgiveness for times you have turned a blind eye to evil, and ask God to help you to hate injustice as He does
- Thank God for a free country where we can speak up in defence of God's law and on behalf of the vulnerable. Pray for the courage to use that freedom well
- Pray for women considering abortion, that they may change their minds and protect their babies instead of killing them
- Thank God for children in your life
- Pray that God will bless Christian foster families with love, compassion, and community support

DISCUSSION QUESTIONS

1. Do you think our constant exposure to news, from local to national to international, contributes to us being able to easily turn a blind eye to suffering? How do you decide what issues to care about?

2. How can we hate suffering without letting it consume us?

3. Do you think praying for the government regularly will impact how we talk about them and their work?

4. Re-read Proverbs 6:16-19 and discuss the other things the Lord hates. Why do you think we sometimes elevate one sin as more serious than others, when these seven seem equal in God's eyes? How can we encourage one another to fight against sin, both in our personal lives and in our lives as citizens of a country?

ISAIAH 40

COMFORT FOR GOD'S PEOPLE
Comfort, comfort my people, says your God.
Speak tenderly to Jerusalem,
  and cry to her
that her warfare is ended,
  that her iniquity is pardoned,
that she has received from the Lord's hand
  double for all her sins.
A voice cries:
"In the wilderness prepare the way of the Lord;
  make straight in the desert a highway for our God.
Every valley shall be lifted up,
  and every mountain and hill be made low;
the uneven ground shall become level,
  and the rough places a plain.
And the glory of the Lord shall be revealed,
  and all flesh shall see it together,
  for the mouth of the Lord has spoken."

THE WORD OF GOD STANDS FOREVER
A voice says, "Cry!"
  And I said, "What shall I cry?"
All flesh is grass,
  and all its beauty is like the flower of the field.
The grass withers, the flower fades

when the breath of the Lord blows on it;
  surely the people are grass.
The grass withers, the flower fades,
  but the word of our God will stand forever.

THE GREATNESS OF GOD

Go on up to a high mountain,
  O Zion, herald of good news;
lift up your voice with strength,
  O Jerusalem, herald of good news;
  lift it up, fear not;
say to the cities of Judah,
  "Behold your God!"
Behold, the Lord God comes with might,
  and his arm rules for him;
behold, his reward is with him,
  and his recompense before him.
He will tend his flock like a shepherd;
  he will gather the lambs in his arms;
he will carry them in his bosom,
  and gently lead those that are with young.
Who has measured the waters in the hollow of his hand
  and marked off the heavens with a span,
enclosed the dust of the earth in a measure
  and weighed the mountains in scales
  and the hills in a balance?
Who has measured the Spirit of the Lord,
  or what man shows him his counsel?
Whom did he consult,

and who made him understand?
Who taught him the path of justice,
and taught him knowledge,
and showed him the way of understanding?
Behold, the nations are like a drop from a bucket,
and are accounted as the dust on the scales;
behold, he takes up the coastlands like fine dust.
Lebanon would not suffice for fuel,
nor are its beasts enough for a burnt offering.
All the nations are as nothing before him,
they are accounted by him as less than nothing and emptiness.
To whom then will you liken God,
or what likeness compare with him?
An idol! A craftsman casts it,
and a goldsmith overlays it with gold
and casts for it silver chains.
He who is too impoverished for an offering
chooses wood that will not rot;
he seeks out a skillful craftsman
to set up an idol that will not move.
Do you not know? Do you not hear?
Has it not been told you from the beginning?
Have you not understood from the foundations of the earth?
It is he who sits above the circle of the earth,
and its inhabitants are like grasshoppers;
who stretches out the heavens like a curtain,
and spreads them like a tent to dwell in;
who brings princes to nothing,
and makes the rulers of the earth as emptiness.
Scarcely are they planted, scarcely sown,

scarcely has their stem taken root in the earth,
when he blows on them, and they wither,
  and the tempest carries them off like stubble.
To whom then will you compare me,
  that I should be like him? says the Holy One.
Lift up your eyes on high and see:
  who created these?
He who brings out their host by number,
  calling them all by name;
by the greatness of his might
  and because he is strong in power,
  not one is missing.
Why do you say, O Jacob,
  and speak, O Israel,
"My way is hidden from the Lord,
  and my right is disregarded by my God"?
Have you not known? Have you not heard?
The Lord is the everlasting God,
  the Creator of the ends of the earth.
He does not faint or grow weary;
  his understanding is unsearchable.
He gives power to the faint,
  and to him who has no might he increases strength.
Even youths shall faint and be weary,
  and young men shall fall exhausted;
but they who wait for the Lord shall renew their strength;
  they shall mount up with wings like eagles;
they shall run and not be weary;
  they shall walk and not faint.

HERALDS OF HOPE

JULIUS VANSPRONSEN
Edmonton, 2019

Suggested song:
DO YOU NOT KNOW, HAVE YOU NOT HEARD?
Scripture reading: **ISAIAH 40**

Tens of thousands of unborn children are killed every year, and our country – its leaders and its citizens – turns a blind eye. We pray, send emails, speak up, march for life, and try to live in a way that shows love for life, but we live in a time when the voice of God is not respected by those who have the power to make decisions about the direction and character of our country.

In times like this we can feel pretty weak and powerless, just like the nation of Israel did when they received the words of the prophecy of Isaiah 40. It may feel like our way is hidden from the

LORD and our right is disregarded by God (Isaiah 40:27). Yet it is in a time like this that Isaiah comes with a message of comfort for the people of God, a message still relevant for us today.

A GOOD SHEPHERD

The church does not have the authority or political influence to ensure that the human right to life is preserved for people of all ages. But that doesn't mean we are to be silent; we are called to lift up our voices, to be heralds of the good news that our world so desperately needs. The good news is that of a sovereign, gracious God, a God who cares. The nations that we consider numerous, and the governments we consider powerful, are as insignificant and incidental to God as a piece of dust on the scales (Isaiah 40:15-17; 23-24). Yet this same God is gentle like a shepherd with little lambs.

The same God who created the oceans and mountains and measures them in His hand like a toy, the LORD Almighty who sits enthroned above the circle of the earth, the most powerful Holy One who calls each of the trillions of stars by name, this God also tends His flock like a shepherd. It is abundantly clear from our text that God Almighty is a God who cares. When the Son of God took on human flesh, He even called Himself the Good Shepherd. This is the God that the world must know!

Our nation might ignore the little ones, and even we might find it easy to forget them, but the LORD is a God who sees, who knows also the babies and children on the earth. Those who believe in the LORD take great comfort in knowing of His love for the little lambs. We rejoice to read that He gathers them in His arms and carries them in His bosom, and gently leads those that are with young (Isaiah 40:11).

A GOD WHO SEES

Knowing that God creates and sees these little ones, we should then desire to show love for them, our neighbours. God created life, forms life in the womb, loves life, honours life. No one is hidden from His view. God so loved the world that He sent His only Son into the world, His Son who is the Life and the source of abundant life.

Although babies in the womb may not hear our voices, we lift our voices so that everyone else may know that the lives of the unborn are not hidden from God's sight. We know our nation will have to give an account, as we all will, and so let the unborn children not be hidden from our sight either, not disregarded by God's people. We are in the world as ambassadors of the Sovereign Creator and His Son Jesus Christ. We march as heralds of the good news that God sees every injustice, and He will make all things right in His timing. He knows the cause of unprotected unborn babies, and He values the life of every human being.

HERALDS OF HOPE

We have been transformed by the grace of God in Jesus Christ, and thanks to this transformation we are also heralds with a message of hope and comfort for mothers who feel overwhelmed by unwanted pregnancies and crushed by the pressures of a society that has accepted murder as a legitimate way to avoid further difficulty. We want these women to know that the LORD, who is the everlasting God, the Creator of the ends of the earth, does not faint or grow weary, and His understanding is unsearchable (Isaiah 40:28). The LORD is a God who gives strength to His people, who can transform others through Jesus Christ, who offers forgiveness and healing to those who come to Him.

While the LORD tells us that He loves life and wants us to protect it, He also reveals that He understands those who don't want to protect life. The LORD's understanding is unsearchable, and the Holy Spirit tells us that our High Priest Jesus Christ is able to sympathize with our weaknesses. There is peace and hope in Jesus because He understands our thoughts, knows our weaknesses, and offers free grace to those who repent and turn to Him. Let us have similar compassion for those who have had abortions and are suffering, those who felt they needed an abortion just to survive, and also those who want the freedom to abort and are belligerent advocates for abortion. They are all hurting people who desperately need the gospel of grace in Jesus Christ. Christians must seek to understand and sympathize in humility, modelling the love and compassion that God has shown to us.

Of course, being sympathetic, supportive, and loving does not mean that we will stop fighting for the lives of the unborn. Although we don't hold hatred toward others in our hearts, we should feel a righteous anger against those who kill unborn children and cover up these heinous acts with confusing and nonsensical language about "reproductive rights." It is right to be angry about injustice and evil.

ON EAGLES' WINGS

When you face opposition, remember the amazing power of the Sovereign LORD who stands behind and before you, the LORD before whom one day every knee will bow. Remember that your strength comes from Him, and that He lifts you up to your task each day! We may be frustrated by the abuse of power in government assemblies and judicial courts, but we know that our God is the Sovereign King who directs the hearts of our rulers (Prov. 21:1), and who can bring princes to nothing (Isaiah 40:23). It is exhausting to continually communicate a message that seems to fall on deaf ears, but we are called to be faithful. Isaiah 40 reminds us that the LORD and everlasting God who sustains us "does not faint or grow weary," and in His strength neither will we.

Sharing the gospel of grace for all who believe in Jesus Christ is worth the difficulty we may face in conveying the truth. If you feel challenged or threatened or afraid when speaking up for justice, remember the picture of the eagles that the Holy Spirit refers to in Isaiah 40. We are told that, when we wait for the LORD, He will give us strength so that we can mount up with wings like eagles, run and not be weary, walk and not faint (40:31). God is on our side, and He is faithful! We are not underdogs who must slink around in weakness and shame. We are the image bearers of God, speaking up for other image bearers. We represent the Sovereign LORD and we simply will not accept society's attempts to silence our voice.

God gives power to the faint and God increases the strength of those who have no might. Live for Him and speak for life with confidence and joy. Let the world know by your actions, your words, and your love about your sovereign God and Father, the One who holds the oceans in His hand and knows the names of each of the stars, and who is also gentle and loving like a shepherd carrying the little sheep close to his chest. May we mount up on eagles' wings as we are carried along by the LORD, and speak of His love to the world.

PRAYER POINTS

- Pray for strength and courage in speaking to others about the need to protect life
- Thank God for His transforming grace in your life and ask Him to give you compassion and love for others
- Acknowledge your own weakness and thank God for promising His strength and energy to carry you through your tasks for the day
- Pray for perseverance and faithfulness to bring the good news of the gospel even when it seems to fall on deaf ears
- Pray that women hurting from abortion will find peace in knowing Jesus
- Pray for opportunities to practice "lifting up your voice" as a herald of the good news

DISCUSSION QUESTIONS

1. Have there been times in your life when you felt God carrying you in His strength during a difficult conversation?

2. Find some Bible texts that speak encouragement for when you are feeling discouraged about not seeing fruit from your work.

3. How does it comfort you to know that Jesus Christ is a High Priest who sympathizes with your weaknesses?

MATTHEW 5:1-16

Seeing the crowds, he went up on the mountain, and when he sat down, his disciples came to him.

And he opened his mouth and taught them, saying:

"Blessed are the poor in spirit, for theirs is the kingdom of heaven."

"Blessed are those who mourn, for they shall be comforted."

"Blessed are the meek, for they shall inherit the earth."

"Blessed are those who hunger and thirst for righteousness, for they shall be satisfied."

"Blessed are the merciful, for they shall receive mercy."

"Blessed are the pure in heart, for they shall see God."

"Blessed are the peacemakers, for they shall be called sons of God."

"Blessed are those who are persecuted for righteousness' sake, for theirs is the kingdom of heaven."

"Blessed are you when others revile you and persecute you and utter all kinds of evil against you falsely on my account. Rejoice and be glad, for your reward is great in heaven, for so they persecuted the prophets who were before you."

"You are the salt of the earth, but if salt has lost its taste, how shall its saltiness be restored? It is no longer good for anything except to be thrown out and trampled under people's feet."

"You are the light of the world. A city set on a hill cannot be hidden. Nor do people light a lamp and put it under a basket, but on a stand, and it gives light to all in the house. In the same way, let your light shine before others, so that they may see your good works and give glory to your Father who is in heaven."

SALT & LIGHT

BEN JOLLIFFE
Ottawa, 2019

Suggested song:
WHO TRUSTS IN GOD, A STRONG ABODE
Scripture reading: **MATTHEW 5:1-16**

One of the major questions that we wrestle with as the church broadly speaking is: What is the relationship of the church to the world around us?

Many of the biblical metaphors for the church — a temple, the body of Christ, and so on — don't address it directly. The metaphors are more concerned with our internal understanding of what we are supposed to become, or they are concerned with how we relate to God and to each other as a community. But the salt and light metaphor in this passage from Matthew, while having some implications for who we are as a church, also orients us towards the outside world.

This is very helpful because we don't exist in a vacuum. The church is not a monastery in the wilderness. We don't live far out in a desert, unbothered by the demands and needs of the world. We interact with our neighbours and our city. We have contact with people who are far from God and believe very different things than the Christian church.

And so, the metaphor of the church as salt and light tells us two very important things about the relationship of the church to the world, and also tells us something fundamental about the nature of the world.

OVERFLOWING BLESSING

Let me take a moment to situate the comments about salt and light. It comes right on the heels of the Beatitudes, or the blessings, that Jesus pronounces in the beginning of the Sermon on the Mount. Jesus tells us:

Blessed are the poor in the spirit for they will inherit the kingdom of God.
Blessed are those who mourn for they shall be comforted.
Blessed are the meek.
Blessed are those who hunger and thirst.
Blessed are the merciful.
Blessed are the peacemakers.
Blessed are the persecuted.

This successive naming of all the kinds of people God blesses leaves you feeling warm and downy soft. But directly out of these statements of blessing comes a section about the responsibility and role of the blessed ones. It is an interesting placement. Jesus wants to emphasize that the blessings carry responsibility. The blessings were never meant to terminate at you, or even on us as a church. The blessings from God are always intended to spill over.

When God blesses Abraham in the book of Genesis, He tells Abraham, "I will make you a great nation, your descendants will be like sand on the seashore, kings will come from your line." And is that the end? No: "And in you all the families of the earth shall be blessed" (Genesis 12:3). The blessings are not hoarded – they don't terminate with Abraham and his immediate family – they overflow to the world.

If you can picture Niagara Falls, you can picture a big horseshoe ring of water, 168,000 cubic metres of water rushing over the top every minute. The flow of water represents God's blessings and love for His people, while the church is a small cup at the bottom. The reality is that we can never hope to contain God's blessings. Our fears about not having enough are unfounded. We will be filled much faster than we can pour out. The blessings of God come with implicit and explicit commands to share those blessings with the world.

Now, let's be honest, if you walked out the doors of your church and meandered down the street asking people the questions, Who does the Christian church exist for? Who are they concerned about? what would they answer? If recent research is accurate, a large percentage of non-churchgoing people think that the church exists only for itself. The perception is that we have our own thing, and it is for the people that go here. We meet our own needs.

And there is an aspect to which that is accurate. The church exists for the nurture and help of the people of God. But it is never supposed to end there. I think this metaphor of salt and light makes that obvious. Salt and light are outward-facing metaphors. Their entire purpose is bound up in being where they are not a majority, where their function will be of some good.

Before we go deeper, a legitimate question to ask is whether Jesus is talking about individual Christians or the church as a whole. Who exactly does Jesus have in mind here? You as a little ol' Christian or all of us as a unit? Though you can certainly understand this metaphor as an individual, I think Jesus has in mind the church when He uses this metaphor. The pronoun in this text is plural. "You" is ambiguous in English; it could refer to the singular or the plural. Here, only the plural is used by Jesus. It would be more obvious if we were reading in French or Greek.

The salt of the earth is a group of people. The light of the world is a group of people. The children's song lyric "this little light of mine, I'm gonna let it shine" is not quite accurate in representing what Jesus is saying here. When Jesus tells us to let our light shine He is saying all of us, as a group, shine together.

This plurality is further reinforced by the second part of verse 14. After telling us that we are the light of the world, He says a city set on a hill cannot be hidden. Jesus probably has in mind a city at night, up on a hill with its torches and lights shining for all to see. One person cannot be a city by themselves. The only way to form a city is with other people. I make this point because surveys indicate that 80% of North Americans believe that you can be a good Christian without going to church. But that is opposed to what Jesus is saying – He is saying it takes a city, a group of people, to form salt and light. You are not a city on a hill all by yourself. The salt and light are to be the people of God together.

With this in mind, there are two things that Jesus is saying using this metaphor, especially as it relates to a watching world: that salt and light oppose, and salt and light preserve.

WHAT SALT AND LIGHT OPPOSE

Where is salt needed? In places of decay, in places of tastelessness, in places that need to be preserved. In the days of Jesus, there was no refrigeration for meats or other foods. The only way to preserve food was by salting it, to prevent bacteria and other nasties from growing. Without salt, there would be decay. And where is light needed? In places of darkness, in places where people are trying to see but cannot, in places of corruption. When we realize where salt and light are found, it brings us to the first thing we want to say about the church as salt and light: the church opposes corruption and decay in every way.

Salt and light, as part of their essence, are sent to places where corruption needs to be opposed, where evil exists, where there is darkness. These are the places the church is specifically called to be. The church is called, by virtue of this metaphor, to all the places where there is corruption. Which, if you begin to think for a moment, is kind of a wide swath of places.

Notice how big of a context Jesus creates. He says you are the salt of the earth. You are the light of the world. Both of these words involve cosmic scope, encompassing not just the spiritual realm or the moral realm but also the physical world, emotional world, social world, economic world, ecological world, the world of work, the world of raising children, the world of education. The church is to be in all of these places, opposing corruption and decay, arresting evil wherever possible.

Noted theologian Fleming Rutledge writes, "The beginning of resistance to evil is not to explain, but to see. Seeing is itself a part of action - seeing evil for what it is... a colossal x factor in creation, a monstrous contradiction, a prodigious negation that must be identified, denounced and opposed wherever it occurs." This is part of the calling of the church.

How do we do that? What does that mean? Opposition happens in two ways, and they are often simultaneous. The first opposition comes in creating a community of holiness, joy, hope and love that resists by example. The second opposition is by actual critique. That might take the form of protests or letters to the editor, but also could be in the form of day-to-day conversations with the people or institutions that you are opposed to.

But it is not enough for us to say to the culture, this is wrong, this is evil. There must be a corresponding example of what the counterculture looks like. To oppose corruption and evil, we need to have something to point to as the alternative. For instance, every election there seems to be a ramping up not just of a debate about ideas and ideologies but also personal attacks, slander, meanness, etc. It is not enough for a church or group of Christians to say - stop that! Stop attacking each other, be more civil. It must also be true that the church is the place where we have honest, respectful dialogue and disagreements. Where opposing opinions are handled in love. Where we learn to forgive each other when we speak meanly and out of turn. This gives legitimacy to our critique.

Another example: classical, historic Christianity opposes abortion, medical assistance in dying, and the rest. But we must not simply oppose this corruption by being loud and obnoxious. For salt to be salty, it needs to be different, not just offensive. For the critique to be robust and strong, there must be the growth of a corresponding culture in the church that doesn't just not abort, but that actively seeks to value and love children. And not just our own children, but all children. To seek a just and good society and city for them to grow up in. To be on the front lines not just of saving pre-born lives, but also of adoption, fostering, education, play groups and whatever else. That is what it means to be salt.

And so, while critiquing what has gone wrong and making an effort to preserve our society, we also create communities of goodness and joy and counterculture, to the glory of God.

Now, let's be honest, we face a few temptations in this area of opposing corruption. The first temptation is to love the creation of a counterculture but not the protest. If you are an average Canadian, you don't like to cause too much trouble. You don't want emotions to run high or voices to be raised above normal volume. We are a live-and-let-live sort of country. I am, and maybe you are too, tempted to cloak my critiques in a polite Canadianness. We are happy to create something beautiful and different but we don't speak out in any distinct way. We don't advocate directly. We don't want to have an honest conversation with someone who really disagrees with us. We don't live in a way that seeks to overcome fear.

But this is not the way God intended it. Salt enters into places of decay and preserves them. It doesn't stand apart. It doesn't create a little salt neighbourhood where all the salty kids only play with other salty kids while they listen to their salty music and wear salty t-shirts. Our refusal to get involved is not us maintaining purity, it is a failure to love. It is a failure to be salt. Salt goes into things that are not salted, and does good there.

Sometimes our love of counterculture but not of protest results in a church that only knows each other, has no friends and contacts outside their church, has no voice in the culture, and refuses all non-essential contact. If you sense some of this in yourself, and I know it is in me, please listen carefully to Jesus' words in verse 13: "If salt loses its taste, how shall its saltiness be restored? It is no longer good for anything except to be thrown out and trampled under people's feet." According to Jesus, the church, when it refuses a prophetic calling to preserve culture and prevent decay, becomes worthless.

The second temptation is the opposite of the first. We love the protest but not the longer work of creating a counterculture. We love to get on Facebook or stand up at a coffee shop or even on Parliament Hill and soapbox, proclaiming all the things that are wrong with the culture. And you may be right, but some of us who love the protest spend so much time there that there is nothing to back it up. There is no society behind you that lives in a radically different way. Your view of children is not any sort of antidote to an abortion mindset. Your political conversations are as biased, one-sided and full of vitriol as everyone else's. You have become hot sauce instead of salt.

Salt provides a different taste. It enhances the food it enters into. It gives a whiff of a better world, a different way of living. Salt must maintain its taste if it hopes to flavour the food. So the Christian church opposes evil and corruption as part of its calling to be salt and light.

WHAT SALT AND LIGHT PRESERVE

As salt makes dishes flavourful and light gives illumination to the people in the house, so Christians must not be totally preoccupied with preventing evil, but must be equally at work doing good. I have been hinting at this already. Light is often used in the Scriptures, not just as a descriptor of Jesus, but also as a way to talk about truth. When light comes into darkness, the Scriptures often speak of truth penetrating into ignorance and lies.

The church's calling of being salt and light involves not just eliminating evil and returning society to neutral, but also of elevating and strengthening what is good and right in our world. Sometimes this involves supporting things that already exist, but other times it involves creating whole new structures and organizations and ways of living as a demonstration of the gospel. In fact, the authors of Scripture write that, in light of God's goodness in creation, we are to enjoy all the things of earth in light of their true purpose and as part of worship to the God who created them. The way that Christians celebrate and enjoy all the good of the earth is intended to be a ministry to all the other people of the earth.

Madeleine L'Engle wrote: "We draw people to Christ by showing them a light that is so lovely that they want with all their heart to know the source of it." 500 years or so earlier, Blaise Pascal, a mathematician, said something similar: "Make Christianity attractive, make it so that good men wish it were true, and then show them that it is." Christianity takes what is good in the world and works to magnify it and make it even better.

Consider getting dressed in a dark room. As you search for socks to wear, you realize that you neglected, as you did the laundry, to put socks in matching pairs. And every sock is a dark colour. How do you determine which is blue and which is black? You must turn on the light and wake up your sleeping spouse. It is only in the presence of the light that you can figure out what is right.

GLORY TO GOD

Remember the context: Christians ought to go into every area of the world, flick on the light switch, and point out what is good and needs to be strengthened, or point out what is missing and start it.

Jesus makes an interesting connection in verse 16 – He says that what happens when salt and light are doing good work is that people see it and give glory to God in heaven. The hope is that in these acts, people understand something about God. But even if they don't, the acts are still good. We are still commanded to do them. We ought to be as creative as we can about bringing justice and goodness to our city.

Temptations, though, exist here as well. For one, we love to create good, but not support good. Christian culture is a bit infamous for taking something good in the culture and ripping it off to create a slightly less good version for all the Christians to enjoy. We have our own t-shirts, our own concerts, our own bracelets, and so on. These things aren't wrong, but if that is all we have, we are missing part of our calling. Our light isn't shining for all the people in the house, it is just in one corner. We are not salting the whole earth, just one pot. We must be people who create good when we can, but also people who support good where it already exists.

WHERE DO WE GET THE STRENGTH TO DO THIS?

First of all, this calling to be salt and light takes an immense amount of wisdom. It requires managing many different relationships with all kinds of people who are privately, and sometimes publicly, opposed to what Christians believe.

Second, this calling to be salt and light takes an immense amount of internal strength. A Christian church must be so secure in who it is to be able to give away resources, money, and time to other organizations while not demanding or expecting anything in return.

Third, it is simply a difficult calling. This metaphor implies the mixing of the church, as both a community and as individuals, with people who are very unlike us and who will challenge us. How do you get the strength to live like this when all your neighbours think you are crazy?

So where do we get all these internal resources from? How do you resist the temptation to hit back? To be as mean as the ones who oppose you? How do we go on creating a good counterculture when we have setback after setback? Well, there is only one place to draw strength and purpose for this calling, and that is the gospel of Jesus Christ.

Notice the tense of the verbs that call us salt and light - You are the salt of the earth. You are the light of the world. This is not something we become, but something that has been done to us. You see, if salt and light was a status that we obtained through hard work, we would have all the reasons in the world to hoard it for ourselves...I have become this great light because I meditated and read my Bible and laboured for many years and now I don't need to share this light with anyone, it might get dimmer! I have worked so hard to become salty and different, I am not just going to go sprinkling it around everywhere, I might lose some of my saltiness!

No, no - Ephesians 5:8 tells us that once we were darkness, but now we are light in the Lord. You. Us. The church. We didn't make ourselves light. God made us light. Once we were not salty, now we have been made into salt. All of this is a gift. We are a tiny cup under a gigantic waterfall. We are so bombarded by grace, so caught up in the blessing of God that it is foolish not to let it spill out of us. It's not about deserving or earning anything – we didn't deserve or earn anything. It's not about being smarter or more moral, that's not why God rescued us.

Jesus is the true light of the world. Jesus is the true salt. He is the one who makes us what we are and if it is a gift then we are simply thankful and humble stewards of the great riches that have been given to us.

May God have mercy on us.

PRAYER POINTS

- Thank God for making you salt and light, and pray for wisdom to live in a way that reflects this reality
- Thank God for His abundant, overflowing blessings in your life that will never run out, and ask for a generous heart to share those blessings freely
- Pray for church unity, that churches may work together as effective salt and light in their communities throughout the world
- Ask God to show you ways you are covering your light, or hoarding your saltiness, when you could be a better witness for the gospel

DISCUSSION QUESTIONS

1. "Jesus wants to emphasize that the blessings carry responsibility." Read through the Beatitudes once more (Matthew 5:2-12), and consider what responsibilities you have in relation to each.

2. What does it mean for your life to know that you are salt and light? Does it make you see your interactions with unbelievers differently?

3. Which of the temptations mentioned resonated more with you – are you more likely to retreat into your counterculture and avoid protest, or more likely to act as hot sauce instead of salt?

4. Discuss this quotation from Blaise Pascal: "Make Christianity attractive, make it so that good men wish it were true, and then show them that it is." What does he mean by making Christianity look attractive? Is there something you can change in your life to "make Christianity more attractive"?

5. "The blessings of God come with implicit and explicit commands to share those blessings with the world." Do you think your neighbourhood would answer similarly to the answers described above, that the church exists for itself? If so, how could you change that perception?

PHILIPPIANS 2:1-13

So if there is any encouragement in Christ, any comfort from love, any participation in the Spirit, any affection and sympathy, complete my joy by being of the same mind, having the same love, being in full accord and of one mind. Do nothing from selfish ambition or conceit, but in humility count others more significant than yourselves. Let each of you look not only to his own interests, but also to the interests of others. Have this mind among yourselves, which is yours in Christ Jesus, who, though he was in the form of God, did not count equality with God a thing to be grasped, but emptied himself, by taking the form of a servant, being born in the likeness of men. And being found in human form, he humbled himself by becoming obedient to the point of death, even death on a cross. Therefore God has highly exalted him and bestowed on him the name that is above every name, so that at the name of Jesus every knee should bow, in heaven and on earth and under the earth, and every tongue confess that Jesus Christ is Lord, to the glory of God the Father.

Therefore, my beloved, as you have always obeyed, so now, not only as in my presence but much more in my absence, work out your own salvation with fear and trembling, for it is God who works in you, both to will and to work for his good pleasure.

A GOD OF CHOICE

JASON VANDER HORST
Victoria, 2018

Suggested song:
LET US OF CHRIST OUR LORD AND SAVIOUR SING
Scripture reading: **PHILIPPIANS 2:1-13**

Words are so important. While they're not the only way in which we communicate, they are essential for the operation of society as we know it. Imagine trying to live without words – it would be chaos!

Words are important; they're also powerful. They convey ideas, thoughts, beliefs, and emotions. The subtle nuances of one or two words can communicate a great deal. Are they "rebels" or "freedom fighters"? Does she spend "lavishly," or "recklessly," or "generously"? Is he "cautious" or "anxious"? You see, words mean something; they have a weight and value that contain power.

When it comes to something controversial – something like the question of the rights of children in the womb – we need to take care in setting the terms and tone of the debate through the words we choose. That's why we have an annual event called the March for Life. As we use our voices to communicate with those who disagree with us, or who simply haven't put much thought into it yet, it's important to communicate that we're for something – we are pro-life. This is not the Anti-Choice or Anti-Abortion March – those terms frame our position in a negative light.

And, such descriptions would not be entirely accurate. The word "choice" is interesting in this context. It's claimed by the other view – they say we are "anti-choice" while they are "pro-choice." But we are pro-choice too! We are pro-many-choices, but we also want unborn children to live in order to make a myriad of choices in their lives: dress, music, clothes, career, spouse, travel, food, home. The right to life is a prerequisite to the right to make choices. We want women to be able to choose not to have an abortion, and to make that choice as easy as possible. Even more: we have a God of choice. You see, the idea of "choice" is a big part of understanding who God is and how He works. In addition to being pro-life, our God is also pro-choice. Let's look at how.

GOD CHOOSES PEOPLE

In Ephesians 1:3-6, we read:

"Blessed be the God and Father of our Lord Jesus Christ, who has blessed us in Christ with every spiritual blessing in the heavenly places, even as he chose us in him before the foundation of the world that we should be holy and blameless before him. In love he predestined us for adoption to himself as sons through Jesus Christ, according to the purpose of his will, to the praise of his glorious grace, with which he has blessed us in the Beloved."

Did you catch that? He chose us – that is, all believers – to be His people. And when did He do this? "Before the foundation of the world." Even before creation! Before this world had been created, the Father made an agreement to give His Son a people to bring glory to the Triune God.

Why would He do that? Because He chose to! The text says, "in accordance with his pleasure and will." He didn't have to. This wasn't forced. God chose to share the glory of eternal blessed life with some of His creatures "freely...to the praise of his glorious grace." As Creator and ruler of all, He could do whatever He pleased, and He was pleased to choose to save some of His creation and promote us to glory. But this was not because of anything in us; we don't earn this promotion to glory.

We can see this quite clearly with Israel in the Old Testament. God chose Abraham to make a people out of him, and God blessed and protected them. When they were on the verge of entering the Promised Land, God reminded His people:

> "You are a people holy to the Lord your God. The Lord your God has chosen you to be a people for his treasured possession, out of all the peoples who are on the face of the earth. It was not because you were more in number than any other people that the Lord set his love on you and chose you, for you were the fewest of all peoples, but it is because the Lord loves you and is keeping the oath that he swore to your fathers, that the Lord has brought you out with a mighty hand and redeemed you from the house of slavery, from the hand of Pharaoh king of Egypt." (Deuteronomy 7:6-8)

Again, did you catch what the text is saying? They had nothing to offer! God treasured His people then, and He treasures His people now, and it has nothing to do with how powerful we are or how capable we are. We have been chosen by Him, and we are loved by Him, simply and purely because He has placed His love and affection upon us, and He is faithful to the promises that He makes.

This has so much application to the pro-life cause. A common argument you'll hear is that "the baby in the womb is not a person." I remember an extended conversation I had once with a member of Planned Parenthood on a city street in Denver. Her whole argument centred on the idea that a baby is not a person. From our perspective, we wonder how they can say this. Clearly, the baby is a person. Well, that depends on how you define "person." In her mind, she defined personhood by function. Are they self-aware? Do they have the ability to create, feel, and love? But you can find animals that qualify under this standard! What makes me a person is not what I do, but what I am. I am created in God's image, and so I am a person. Babies in the womb are created in God's image, and so they are persons too – and hear this, it's so important we understand this next part – persons even though they have nothing to offer!

God does not make His choice to love us based on our abilities, and so we ought not to make our choices about babies dependent on their abilities. They are worthy of our love simply by being human! The same is true for any women or girls considering abortion. There are any number of reasons why a person considers aborting their child. Often, the situation is quite messy and broken. But we ought to help them – regardless of whether or not they have anything to offer us, or there is anything desirable about them or their story. To choose to love them is a right imitation of the God who freely chose to love us, in the richness of His grace.

GOD OFFERS HIS PEOPLE A CHOICE

God chooses His people, and He also offers them a choice. In Deuteronomy, after affirming his love for Israel, God laid down His law. He commanded the people to carefully keep it all, and He tells them that if they keep it, they will receive the blessing of land and prosperity. If they fail to keep it, they will receive the curse of famine, infertility, distress and exile. So, He left them with a choice: "See, I have set before you today life and good, death and evil. … Now choose! Choose life!" (Deut. 30:15, 19) If you're at all familiar with the biblical story, you know how that went. The choice was held out for them, but they could never attain it. The guilt and corruption of sin had infected all humanity, and so the Israelites were doomed to failure. And so, because God's people could not choose life on their own, God chose to die.

GOD CHOSE TO DIE

God's love was so great that He chose to die for us. We have nothing to offer – on the contrary, we messed up big time. Yet He showed us His love in Jesus as He sent His only Son; He didn't spare him, but He gave Him up for us all. All that we have is from Him.

Philippians 2 reminds us of how greatly Jesus humbled Himself. He willingly set aside the glory and the comfort of heaven to come to earth as a man – the Lord of all creation became a servant! And not just any man, but a man despised and rejected, a man of many sorrows. His humility and love took Him all the way to a cross, on which He died the death of a cursed man. He took our curse on Himself so that we would be freed from it. This is amazing love! How can it be? That the King of all creation would die for me? For you?

If we understand this, it's pretty clear what our response needs to be.

WE NEED TO CHOOSE

If you don't know Jesus – if this is all new to you – you need to choose to repent and believe. To turn away from sin and doing things your own way, to turn to Him, looking for your righteousness and life. If the Scripture readings and this message have made anything clear, hopefully it's this: there is grace! Maybe you've had an abortion in the past, or maybe you've pressured someone into one. God's grace is sufficient for you. Even for the lawmakers and practitioners of abortion – God's grace can reach them. After all, God reached out and transformed Saul, one of the worst persecutors of the early church. Once God's grace was worked in Saul's life, he was transformed into a new man. As the apostle Paul, he became the foremost preacher of the gospel in the early church.

If you are a believer and you do know Jesus Christ, you and I need to choose daily to follow Him. To be a Christian is to be a Christ-follower. We are united to Him by our faith, and so we are to live out of that union. This means, first and foremost, that we love as He loved. Freely! Extravagantly! Fully! And there's something very notable about the way He loved. Have you noticed? He loved those who were vulnerable. Yes, He loved all sorts of people – but particularly the vulnerable: women and children and public sinners who were maligned by others, people who were not wealthy or influential, who had little to no prospects and who could offer Him nothing in return except for their own love. This is what we are called to do. To love the vulnerable. To love the baby in the womb. To love the woman or girl in a desperate situation, feeling the pressure to abort and at a loss to see any other option.

There is a lot that can be said about the pro-life cause. The debates can get complex and highly political. I don't believe it's my role as a minister to speak to the specifics of government policies. But it is my role to proclaim the truth of God's Word as it applies to protecting human life and loving the vulnerable. The truth of God's Word is that the child in the womb is to be protected and loved. The truth of God's Word is that we are to support and love those women who are in need. God's Word tells us to consider others as more significant than ourselves, and to look to their interests in addition to our own; to be selfless rather than selfish, always remembering the example of our Saviour, who laid down His life for us.

God has loved us so richly, so freely, so graciously! Since God has so loved us, let us love our fellow church members, and let us show love to all members of our communities, from the greatest to the least.

PRAYER POINTS

- Praise God for his free gift of grace and love
- Ask God to give you opportunity to love the vulnerable, to place people on your path to love and to open your eyes to them and their need
- Think of areas in your life where you are prone to self-reliance or trusting your own wisdom. Repent from your sin and turn again to Jesus for all that you need
- Pray that you might have the words when needed to give a defence for what you believe

DISCUSSION QUESTIONS

1. How do God's choices impact the choices we make as His creation?

2. Loving freely can be difficult, as it sets us up for potential hurt and loss. Consider the hurt God has endured due to our persistent sin and unfaithfulness, and reflect on how you can love freely in His strength. How can you show this love to those who seem undeserving?

3. Do you think it's the role of Christians and Christian leaders to get involved in politics? How do you view the distinction between church and state, particularly on the issue of abortion?

4. Often our identity is tied to something other than, or in addition to, our relationship to God. This misplaced identity can impact various transitions in our life, such as losing a job, becoming a parent, becoming an empty nester, reaching retirement, losing our mobility, etc. Discuss how we can meet transitions more gracefully when we understand and treasure our worth in Christ, and His choosing of us.

5. How can we show that we honour life as inherently valuable regardless of someone's ability or status? For example, when we meet someone new, what can we ask besides "What do you do?"

HABAKKUK 1:1-2:3 (NIV)

The prophecy that Habakkuk the prophet received.

HABAKKUK'S COMPLAINT

How long, Lord, must I call for help,
  but you do not listen?
Or cry out to you, "Violence!"
  but you do not save?
Why do you make me look at injustice?
  Why do you tolerate wrongdoing?
Destruction and violence are before me;
  there is strife, and conflict abounds.
Therefore the law is paralyzed,
  and justice never prevails.
The wicked hem in the righteous,
  so that justice is perverted.

THE LORD'S ANSWER

"Look at the nations and watch—
  and be utterly amazed.
For I am going to do something in your days
  that you would not believe,
  even if you were told.
I am raising up the Babylonians,
  that ruthless and impetuous people,
who sweep across the whole earth
  to seize dwellings not their own.
They are a feared and dreaded people;
  they are a law to themselves

and promote their own honor.
Their horses are swifter than leopards,
fiercer than wolves at dusk.
Their cavalry gallops headlong;
their horsemen come from afar.
They fly like an eagle swooping to devour;
they all come intent on violence.
Their hordes advance like a desert wind
and gather prisoners like sand.
They mock kings
and scoff at rulers.
They laugh at all fortified cities;
by building earthen ramps they capture them.
Then they sweep past like the wind and go on—
guilty people, whose own strength is their god."

HABAKKUK'S SECOND COMPLAINT

Lord, are you not from everlasting?
My God, my Holy One, you will never die.
You, Lord, have appointed them to execute judgment;
you, my Rock, have ordained them to punish.
Your eyes are too pure to look on evil;
you cannot tolerate wrongdoing.
Why then do you tolerate the treacherous?
Why are you silent while the wicked
swallow up those more righteous than themselves?
You have made people like the fish in the sea,
like the sea creatures that have no ruler.
The wicked foe pulls all of them up with hooks,
he catches them in his net,

he gathers them up in his dragnet;
  and so he rejoices and is glad.
Therefore he sacrifices to his net
    and burns incense to his dragnet,
  for by his net he lives in luxury
    and enjoys the choicest food.
Is he to keep on emptying his net,
  destroying nations without mercy?
I will stand at my watch
  and station myself on the ramparts;
I will look to see what he will say to me,
  and what answer I am to give to this complaint.

THE LORD'S ANSWER

Then the Lord replied:
"Write down the revelation
  and make it plain on tablets
  so that a herald may run with it.
For the revelation awaits an appointed time;
  it speaks of the end
  and will not prove false.
Though it linger, wait for it;
  it will certainly come
  and will not delay.

HOW LONG, O LORD? WRESTLING, WORSHIPPING AND WAITING IN PRAYER

MATT KINGSWOOD
Ottawa, 2018

Suggested song: **THE PRAYER OF HABAKKUK**
Scripture reading: **HABAKKUK 1:1-2:3 (NIV)**

In Romans 12:12, in the middle of the chapter describing what it means to live as a living sacrifice in view of God's mercies, the apostle Paul says, "Be joyful in hope, patient in affliction, faithful in prayer." Every Christian is thus called to be "faithful," or steadfast, in prayer.

Prayer, in the name of Jesus Christ, motivated and molded by the proclamation of God's Word, is vital in every circumstance and situation of life. In Acts 4:24, when the apostles had been released from prison, we read that after the apostles reported all that had happened to them, prayer was the supernatural reflex-response of the church: "When they heard this, they lifted their voices together to God and said, 'Sovereign Lord,...'" John Bunyan once said, "You can do more than pray, after you have prayed, but you cannot do more than pray until you have prayed."

The book of Habakkuk is a book of prayer. In fact, it is a book which records three prayers and God's two answers to those prayers. In this prophecy consisting of collected prayers, then, we have the inspired, infallible record of a believer's experience in prayer. By God's grace this part of Scripture will help us today in our praying.

WRESTLING IN PRAYER

The first thing we see in the opening lines of this book is a believer wrestling in prayer. The prophet's own name, "Habakkuk," comes from the Hebrew word that means "embrace." Some have helpfully suggested that the "embracing" here in chapter 1 has the sense of a wrestler in an embrace with an opponent, grappling with the one whom he is contending with. Habakkuk was wrestling with God's providence, wrestling with what he saw happening around him, and God's place in it.

In the NIV, editors have inserted the heading "Habakkuk's complaint." That doesn't sound very positive, does it? It sounds like an accusation. Complaining about our circumstances is a very easy thing to do, but it is not a Christian thing to do. "Do everything without complaining or arguing," Paul wrote in Philippians 2. But is Habakkuk complaining in the sense we would use that word? Is he moaning and groaning, even whining perhaps?

To see Habakkuk's prayer as "complaining" in our common use of the word would be superficial and misleading. Habakkuk's heart, reflected in his prayer, is better considered along the lines of what Peter said about Lot: "a righteous man, who was distressed by the depraved conduct of the lawless...tormented in his righteous soul by the lawless deeds he saw and heard" (2 Peter 2:7-8, NIV). Or think of the psalmist in Psalm 119:136, who writes, "Streams of tears flow from my eyes, for your law is not obeyed."

We should be distressed and tormented by sin. We should not sit easy with it. Our weapons are not the weapons of this world, but we do spiritually wrestle with the presence of sin. In every age in history, the people of God know what Paul said in Ephesians 6:12 is true: "For we do not wrestle against flesh and blood, but against the rulers, against the authorities, against the cosmic powers over this present darkness, against the spiritual forces of evil in the heavenly places."

But what specifically was happening in the days of Habakkuk that caused him to wrestle in prayer? We get a good sense of the situation from Habakkuk's prayer itself. Look at the words he uses - violence, injustice, wrong, destruction, strife, conflict. The picture he paints is of a culture in serious trouble and decline. There have been, and are today, many places in the world just like the society Habakkuk described. We don't have to look far to see a comparable situation here in the West. We could easily go through each descriptive word here and find parallels to today. The further our culture wants to get away from God and His Word, the more of this we will see.

Habakkuk mentions violence. A recent news article began with these words: "Road rage, air rage, office rage, desk rage, work rage, bike rage, ... rage is the word of the moment." We see so much domestic violence. Our streets are places of violence. Too often we hear about tragic violence in the spate of mass shootings and other horrific attacks. We lament the hidden, sanitized violence of abortion, along with the rationalized violence of euthanasia.

Habakkuk was dismayed that the legal system of his day was paralyzed...literally, it had "grown numb." Justice did not prevail. Many have accurately characterized our courts today with the same critique; increasingly it seems as though we just have a legal system, not a justice system.

But notice something striking: verse 4 begins with "therefore." We might have thought it would be reversed: "Justice never prevails; therefore violence, strife and conflict abound." But here it is stated the other way around: "[T]here is strife and conflict abounds. Therefore, the law is paralyzed." What is the implication? When a society grows in wickedness, the culture affects the courts. Citizens, legislators and judges can become morally numbed.

This was Habakkuk's situation. There is nothing new under the sun. Technology has changed, but as Martyn Lloyd-Jones once observed, whether people travel 4 mph or 400 mph, they do the same things when they get there. Fallen human nature has never evolved into righteousness and will not do so no matter how strongly secular humanism believes it will.

To make matters worse, our text describes a situation not in a nearby nation, but among God's people, in the church. Sadly, we too can see much that is unbiblical and ungodly in the professing Christian church. As Jesus taught us, we always must begin with the logs in our own eyes, as individuals and as the Church.

However, as bad as it was, the presence of these societal plagues is not really the pith of his prayer here. Note the questions crying out from Habakkuk's heart: In verse 2 he asks, How long? And in verse 3, Why? Habakkuk is wrestling not just with these evils themselves, but with God's seeming silence. As we listen in on Habakkuk's prayer, we are picking up his struggle midstream. He has obviously already spent a long time calling out for help, crying out in prayer. But he can see no answer. His patience in prayer is being tested. And it seems even the prophet is breaking down. Look at his conclusions:

"How long, O LORD, must I call for help, but you do not listen?" He accuses God of inattention.

"Or cry out to you, "Violence!" but you do not save?" He charges the Most High with inactivity! Habakkuk likely thought this silence from God only encouraged sinfulness, similar to the words of the psalmist in Psalm 94:7: "They say, 'The LORD does not see; the God of Jacob pays no heed.'"

What a challenge it can be for the people of God to wrestle with seemingly unanswered prayer! Year by year goes by, with no noticeable change. But we live by faith, not by sight. And we must pray by faith and not by sight. Even in his struggle with God's seeming silence, Habakkuk was a good theologian. He knows his God. It is especially because of his good biblical understanding of God that Habakkuk wrestles. It is because we know that God is sovereign that the "why" questions loom even larger to us.

But if we are praying in Christ and through Christ, we know: "The LORD has heard my cry for mercy; the LORD accepts my prayer" (Psalm 6:9). And we trust the call to "Cast all your anxiety on him because he cares for you" (1 Peter 5:7).

Look closely at the text: Habakkuk knows who is in control. In verse 3 he asks, "Why DO YOU MAKE ME look at injustice?" And then, where the NIV translates "why do you tolerate wrong," it can be translated instead "and cause me to look on wickedness?" In the Hebrew these are causative forms of the verbs. Habakkuk knows God is ultimately in control. He traces his situation back to God's hand. It is really only those who know God is sovereign who wrestle as Habakkuk does here.

Habakkuk, as a believer, did wrestle. We also wrestle as we consider the world, the church and our own lives. We, too, have our own "How longs?", our own "Why?" questions. But along with Habakkuk, whatever our wrestling is, it must never be separated from our worshipping.

WORSHIPPING IN PRAYER

How was Habakkuk worshipping? Well, he was praying. His complaint was a prayer. He didn't just grumble to himself. He didn't complain to those around him. He didn't simply try to take matters into his own hands. He worshipped God by turning to God in prayer. Theologian B. B. Warfield once said that Reformed theology is "Christianity on its knees." True prayer is an act of worship, a testimony that God is sovereign and that only He can truly help and change this world and those in it.

In the prayer beginning in verse 12, we see Habakkuk's worship of God. Habakkuk had much in his heart, many thoughts on his mind, but notice how he began here in prayer. He begins with worship. He acknowledges the attributes and purposes of God:

O LORD, he says, addressing God as *Yahweh*, employing the personal name of the covenant God of His people (Exodus 3:14).

Everlasting God, he prays. God is eternal. He is infinitely above the twists and turns of human history. He is the God who knows the end from the beginning (Isaiah 46:10).

My Holy One, he proclaims, worshipping the God who is holy in His essence, above and beyond all that is created, holy in attributes and character, as separate from sin as light is from darkness. But note also the personal confession of faith: My Holy One. Habakkuk's God is not distant or abstract, but personal and intimate.

The Rock. Habakkuk confesses God as a solid, stable, secure foundation.

Habakkuk began his second prayer with worship. He began the way Jesus taught His disciples to pray, "Hallowed be Thy name." It is right to begin with worship as we pray, to ground our prayers on the solid foundation of God's being, character, and gracious acts.

We must worship God in light of His holiness, and in light of His saving purpose for His people in this world (verse 12 – "we will not die"). That was true of the nation of Israel until Messiah came, and it always has been true of everyone who calls on the name of the Lord, everyone who looks to Christ with saving faith.

We know as Christians that God is in control: He has foreordained whatever comes to pass (Ephesians 1:11). While that truth may initially seem to increase our burden, the struggle to understand, we must rest in the knowledge that God is more holy, wise and merciful than any of us. No matter what the outward circumstances, the worshipping believer can say with Habakkuk in Chapter 3:18, "YET will I rejoice in the Lord, I will be joyful in God my Saviour."

We must always lift up our eyes to the Holy nature of our unchanging God, and to the resurrected and ascended Lord Jesus Christ, to the convicting, convincing work of the Holy Spirit, and we must continue to worship as we wrestle, because the righteous will live by faith.

WAITING IN PRAYER

When wrestling in prayer mingles with worshipping in prayer, it should encourage us to be waiting in prayer. Waiting in prayer is a major theme in Habakkuk, and a calling for all believers. Psalm 27:14 reminds us to "Wait for the LORD; be strong and take heart and wait for the LORD."

Habakkuk lays out his heart before God and in 2:1 says, "I will stand at my watch and station myself on the ramparts; I will look to see what he will say to me, and what answer I am to give to this complaint."

And he gets an answer. As God works out His decree in providence, He encourages Habakkuk in 2:3, "The revelation awaits an appointed time…though it linger, wait for it." We can be impatient, perhaps especially when we think God is tolerating things He shouldn't. But if we are in fact praying to GOD, then we should also be content to submit to God and wait patiently. God is holy and His timing is holy and perfect. As we wait in prayer we should always be hopeful. God Himself says that His answer to Habakkuk would be unexpected!

In World War II, a secret project overseen by Winston Churchill was named "Project Habakkuk." It was the plan for a special warship. A prototype was actually built in Alberta. What was special about this ship was that it was basically made out of ice, actually a mixture of wood pulp and ice, called "Pykecrete" after its inventor Geoffrey Pyke. But the name of the project was based on Habakkuk 1:5: "Look…and be utterly amazed. For I am going to do something in your days that you would not believe, even if you were told."

"Habakkuk," says God, "prepare to be amazed!" God actually uses the same word twice for emphasis - watch and you will be amazingly amazed! The true and living God is the God who does wonders! The prophet had charged God with inattention and indifference – "How long, O LORD, must I call for help, but you do not listen? Or cry out to you, "Violence!" but you do not save?" How that prayer must have sounded in the ear of the Almighty! I do not save?! He is the God who saves! Since Adam fell into sin, to the time the world was filled with violence in the days of Noah, to the time of Abraham, Isaac and Jacob, to the time of Moses and the Exodus, through the times of the Judges and Kings, right up unto Habakkuk's day, the Lord had been saving His people!

And, in the fullness of time centuries after Habakkuk prayed, God brought about a great and mighty wonder, the truly amazing thing we would not have believed unless God Himself told us. God, rich in love and mercy, did not spare His own Son, but gave Him up for us all, while we were yet sinners! (Romans 8:32) And amazingly, yet in perfect righteousness, it was at the cross that God was indeed silent. It was then that His eyes, too pure to look on evil, turned away from His own Son, the Lamb of God – away from the imputed sin and guilt of the Church laid on Jesus. "My God, my God, why have you forsaken me? Why are you so far from saving me, so far from the words of my groaning?" (Psalm 22:1)

God did an amazing thing in Christ to save His people. How can we not be hopeful for lesser, but still amazing, things? Our God is a God who is able to do exceedingly, abundantly above all that we ask or think (Ephesians 3:20). In sovereign power and grace, He can bring repentance and revival to the church and to nations today, if He should so ordain.

But sometimes God answers with the discipline of His people before He answers with deliverance for His people. Verse 5 encourages us to be hopeful, but even more it should teach us to be humble as we wait in prayer. In Habakkuk's day, God raised up the Babylonians to discipline His people. That is how He answered the wrestling prayer of the prophet. As we wait in prayer against injustice in our day, God may choose to answer us very differently than we might expect, but yet for His glory and our good.

In answer to our prayers, God may have dealings with the citizens and government of our country. Because we are called to love our neighbour as we love ourselves, we pray that those would be dealings of mercy and grace, bringing forgiveness and righteousness through repentance and faith in Christ. But He may do something else as we wait, in order to change us, in order to grow and sanctify His Church. "The Lord is not slow in keeping his promise, as some understand slowness. He is patient with you, not wanting anyone to perish, but everyone to come to repentance." (2 Peter 3:9)

It is important and right to speak out for the weak, the helpless, the voiceless. It is right to call the government to remember the law of God and its calling from God (Romans 13). But Habakkuk reminds us that God answers prayer in ways that display His holiness, not only in judgment but also in saving and sanctifying His people. We must be humble as we wait in prayer. We must not just go looking for judgment on others, but hopefully and humbly pleading for mercy, for ourselves and for others.

Our country needs righteous laws. But above all, our country needs the gospel. In the New Testament, the apostle Paul quotes from Habakkuk 1. In Acts 13:38 and following we read:

> "I want you to know that through Jesus the forgiveness of sins is proclaimed to you. Through him everyone who believes is justified from everything you could not be justified from by the law of Moses. Take care that what the prophets have said does not happen to you: "Look, you scoffers, wonder and perish, for I am going to do something in your days that you would never believe, even if someone told you."

It is undeniable that our nation has sin that provokes the Holy God. In fact, we all have sin that needs to be dealt with. The church in Canada has sin that needs to be dealt with. The only ultimate answer, the only good news for sinners, is the Messiah who in Habakkuk's day was yet to come, the Messiah who for us has come, and is coming again: Jesus the Christ.

So, as we wrestle, worship and wait in prayer, we say with Habakkuk (3:2), "LORD, I have heard of your fame; I stand in awe of your deeds, LORD. Repeat them in our day, in our time make them known; in wrath remember mercy."

PRAYER POINTS

- Worship God as LORD, Holy One, everlasting God, and Rock
- Pray for patience in God's timing and trust in His purposes
- Cry out for mercy for yourself and for our nation, and humility to know your own sin
- Pray for revival in the hearts of God's people and for that to impact the culture around us for the glory of God
- Pray through the prayers of Habakkuk, and thank God for this prophecy of answered prayers
- Ask God to help you be persistent in wrestling in prayer, even when the answer is not what you were hoping it would be

DISCUSSION QUESTIONS

1. Do you wrestle in prayer? Do you consistently pray for the same thing day after day, week after week, year after year? What kind of things are you more likely to pray for in this way?

2. How do you use prayer as an opportunity to worship?

3. Read through the entire book of Habakkuk and reflect on the interaction we see between the prophet and the God he serves. How can this book encourage us to approach God with everything on our hearts?

4. What circumstances have happened in your life where you felt God was using a period of waiting to teach you something?

5. How can we pair hopefulness in prayer (trusting in God's power and deliverance) with humility (accepting that the answer may not be what we want)?

6. How do you pray for others? Do you pray *with* others when they share a struggle, or tell them you will pray *for* them?

PSALM 119:129-136

Your testimonies are wonderful;
  therefore my soul keeps them.
The unfolding of your words gives light;
  it imparts understanding to the simple.
I open my mouth and pant,
  because I long for your commandments.
Turn to me and be gracious to me,
  as is your way with those who love your name.
Keep steady my steps according to your promise,
  and let no iniquity get dominion over me.
Redeem me from man's oppression,
  that I may keep your precepts.
Make your face shine upon your servant,
  and teach me your statutes.
My eyes shed streams of tears,
  because people do not keep your law.

LUKE 19:41-44

And when he drew near and saw the city, he wept over it, saying, "Would that you, even you, had known on this day the things that make for peace! But now they are hidden from your eyes. For the days will come upon you, when your enemies will set up a barricade around you and surround you and hem you in on every side and tear you down to the ground, you and your children within you. And they will not leave one stone upon another in you, because you did not know the time of your visitation."

MY EYES SHED STREAMS OF TEARS

GEORGE VAN POPTA
Ottawa, 2017

Suggested song: **PSALM 130**
Scripture reading: **PSALM 119:129-136, LUKE 19:41-44**

Psalm 119 is a masterpiece of Hebrew poetry. It is an acrostic poem consisting of 22 stanzas matching the 22 letters of the Hebrew alphabet. Each stanza is made up of 8 verses. Each of the 8 verses of the first stanza begins with the first letter of the Hebrew alphabet, while the 8 verses of the second stanza start with the second letter, and so on right to the end. Perfect order with iron discipline resulting in beautiful poetry.

Each line in one way or another speaks about the beauty and perfection of God's Word. Using all the different synonyms available, the poet speaks through this long psalm about the law of God. He refers to the Word of God, the law, instruction, precepts, testimonies, commandments, etc. He takes each of those words and works them out further.

The author of Psalm 119 is anonymous. When I say "anonymous" I only mean that we are not told who the human author of the Psalm was. We know who the divine author is: the Holy Spirit. Like all of Scripture, Psalm 119 is the Word of God. But the Holy Spirit inspired a man to write this psalm, and from it we can learn that his time, society, and culture was not much different from ours.

THE POET WEPT

It was a strange world. By that I mean that the author of the psalm felt like a stranger in it. He was an alien – a resident alien, yet an alien. Together with people who were like him, he felt estranged from the world. There were others who, like him, were loyal to God. He wrote here and there in Psalm 119 about these kindred spirits: "I am a companion of all who fear you, of those who keep your precepts" (verse 63), and "Those who fear you shall see me and rejoice, because I have hoped in your word." (verse 74)

So the poet had his compatriots in the faith. But he lived in a climate dominated by religious skeptics. He spoke about people who had, by their indifference, made void the Word of God. There were on the one hand those who were non-committal, "half and half" people who limped along with two opinions. On the other hand, there were those who were thoroughly profane and godless, completely wicked, and who lay in wait to destroy those who followed the Lord. There were those in his society who had derision and contempt for him, who slandered him, who smeared his name. Even the authorities persecuted him. Some of the ones in power were openly apostate and godless. The pressure he felt was murderous.

The human author of the psalm speaks about his youth. He was sensitive to scorn. He felt isolated, small and despised, drained of vitality and dried up and shattered like a piece of broken pottery. At one time he is saddened by it all, and at another time infuriated by what he sees and experiences, reacting now with hot indignation, now with disgust, and now with a river of tears. What bothers him the most is not the scorn and persecution that he experiences. No, what bothers him the most is that God is dishonoured and His Word is ignored and ridiculed. This was the problem in society during the time Psalm 119 was written. Even the leadership elite persecuted those who wanted simply to live according to the Word of God.

What's the problem today? About the same as it was then, wouldn't you say? The Word of God is either ignored or scorned, and even the leadership elite persecute those who want to live by the Word. Some of you have experienced this firsthand. At university you have had your pro-life clubs scorned and ridiculed, and even shut down. You have had to deal with pro-choice students, who spit on your signs and tear up the pink and blue flags you so meaningfully planted, and who get away with it. It seems there are no repercussions for them, while your freedoms are increasingly limited.

When the poet saw this happening around him, streams of tears flowed from his eyes. He wept a river of tears because God's law was not obeyed. We join with our brothers and sisters of the Old Testament and cry a river of tears because God's law is not obeyed.

In relation to abortion, we think especially of the sixth commandment: You shall not kill. Every time there is an abortion, the sixth commandment is broken. About 100,000 times per year in Canada, this commandment of God is not obeyed, and because of that we shed 100,000 streams of tears. It's like a dam burst wide open, and streams of tears flow from our eyes.

JESUS WEPT

We are not the only ones who cry about this disregard for God's law. There was someone else, and His name was Jesus. He wept at sin, and the brokenness it caused. He wept at the grave of Lazarus (John 11). He wept with indignation, as the original Greek has it. Why with indignation? Because death was the result of sin – the wages of sin is death. When Jesus was confronted by that brokenness, He wept.

There is another recorded time when Jesus wept—when he wept over Jerusalem (Luke 19:41).

At the beginning of Passion week, as He was approaching Jerusalem, Jesus wept over the city and said, "If...you had only known...what would bring you peace—but now it is hidden from your eyes." As He spoke of the destruction that would come upon the city, He wept.

WE WEEP

As fellow children of God, we are right to weep at the brokenness caused by sin. A country, a province, a city that ignores the Word of God, that calls evil good and good evil, cannot expect anything but judgment and destruction. But to think about the prospect of judgment and destruction from the hand of God is to bring a person to weeping a river of tears.

Today we should weep a river of tears because of how God's law is not kept. Whatever the law forbids, man wants to do, and what the law commands, man does not want to do.

But when we speak of man—mankind—we need to start with ourselves. I weep a river of tears because of my sin, and because of how I do not obey the law of God. I need to repent from my sins and disobedience. Only when I stand before God naked with shame because of my sin can I also begin to speak about the sin of my fellow citizens, and of my country. It is also when I repent of my sin that a wonderful thing happens. The blood of Jesus Christ washes over me and I come to know and experience the full forgiveness of all my sins. And, dear friends, that is not just for me, and it is not just for you. It is for all who look to Jesus Christ and find in Him salvation. This is the message that goes out to the people of our land: if only they would repent and look to Jesus for salvation, if only they would love the Word of God, they could also experience this full forgiveness. With Jesus we weep, "If only you had known what would bring you peace..."

And so, dear friends, we speak up in defence of life. We volunteer at local pregnancy care centres. We vote for and support leaders who protect life. We love our children and the children of others. And we quietly march down the streets of the city as those who have been redeemed from their sins by the blood and Spirit of Christ.

We shed our tears because the commandment of God is utterly rejected. We shed our tears because the leaders of our country reject the Word of God and the gospel of the Lord Jesus Christ. We shed our tears in solidarity with the 100,000 lives snuffed out before they saw the light of life. And we try to show our neighbours that there is a better way to live, a way that brings peace, that is, the way of Jesus Christ.

We weep in solidarity with our Lord, who wept at the brokenness caused by sin, who wept over a disobedient city and because of the impending destruction. Let us pray for our country and for strength in our task as witnesses to Jesus Christ our Saviour.

PRAYER POINTS

- Pray for a heart that is grieved by sin and brokenness, a heart more like God's own
- Thank God for fellow believers, compatriots in the faith, who can help you stand strong
- Pray for the city or town where you live, that God would be merciful and grant revival
- Confess your sins and praise God for His gracious salvation
- Pray for wisdom to live a God-honouring life, a life that points others to Christ, that you might be used as an effective witness in God's kingdom

DISCUSSION QUESTIONS

1. Do we weep for sin and mourn over the brokenness it causes? How can we balance sincere repentance and conversion with the joy we have in knowing our salvation is secure?

2. Think of examples in today's culture where evil is called good, and good is called evil.

3. Do you sometimes think times are worse now than they used to be? Is this a biblical view?

4. Read Romans 7:7-25. Do you identify with Paul's struggle here? How does knowledge of the law help us? How does self-examination help us to better love both God and our neighbour?

5. Does thinking of abortion as a crime against the sixth commandment make you more willing to speak out against it? Or do you find it hard to view abortion as murder?

PSALM 139

To the choirmaster. A Psalm of David.

O Lord, you have searched me and known me!
You know when I sit down and when I rise up;
  you discern my thoughts from afar.
You search out my path and my lying down
  and are acquainted with all my ways.
Even before a word is on my tongue,
  behold, O Lord, you know it altogether.
You hem me in, behind and before,
  and lay your hand upon me.
Such knowledge is too wonderful for me;
  it is high; I cannot attain it.
Where shall I go from your Spirit?
  Or where shall I flee from your presence?
If I ascend to heaven, you are there!
  If I make my bed in Sheol, you are there!
If I take the wings of the morning
  and dwell in the uttermost parts of the sea,
even there your hand shall lead me,
  and your right hand shall hold me.
If I say, "Surely the darkness shall cover me,
  and the light about me be night,"
even the darkness is not dark to you;
  the night is bright as the day,
  for darkness is as light with you.
For you formed my inward parts;
  you knitted me together in my mother's womb.

I praise you, for I am fearfully and wonderfully made.
Wonderful are your works;
  my soul knows it very well.
My frame was not hidden from you,
when I was being made in secret,
  intricately woven in the depths of the earth.
Your eyes saw my unformed substance;
in your book were written, every one of them,
  the days that were formed for me,
  when as yet there was none of them.
How precious to me are your thoughts, O God!
  How vast is the sum of them!
If I would count them, they are more than the sand.
  I awake, and I am still with you.
Oh that you would slay the wicked, O God!
  O men of blood, depart from me!
They speak against you with malicious intent;
  your enemies take your name in vain.
Do I not hate those who hate you, O Lord?
  And do I not loathe those who rise up against you?
I hate them with complete hatred;
  I count them my enemies.
Search me, O God, and know my heart!
  Try me and know my thoughts!
And see if there be any grievous way in me,
  and lead me in the way everlasting!

WHAT MAKES PEOPLE SPECIAL?

BEN SCHOOF
Victoria, 2017

Suggested song: **PSALM 8**
Scripture reading: **PSALM 139**

What is so special about human beings? What makes us so different? Especially when it comes to the current euthanasia debate, this is an important question. We have no issue with putting down a dog with a terminal illness, or ending the life of a horse that is in severe pain. In fact, most would consider it compassionate! So why not human beings? What makes us so special?

To understand what makes human beings unique from animals, we have to go back to the beginning – to the creation account in Genesis 1 and 2. What we learn there is expanded on by David in Psalm 139.

When we study these texts, we learn that what makes us special is not really about us. It's not who we are that makes us special, it's instead about the God who made us. That ought to take away any sense of pride we might have in ourselves and leave us instead with praise and adoration for the God who made us.

That is what Psalm 139 is about. It is a well-known Psalm which covers many different wonderful things about God and His relationship to people. But in the end, it is a psalm of adoration to God. The first six verses contain wonder at God's omniscience, that He knows everything. The next six verses contain praise of God's omnipresence, that He is everywhere. The third section of six verses, which we will spend most of our time with now, contains adoration for God's amazing creative power. And the last section is about God's holiness. The whole psalm is all about God, about what He has done and continues to do.

SO, WHAT MAKES US SO SPECIAL?

I'm guessing that every Christian, including our little children, know the story of creation well, how God created everything just by speaking. "Let there be light," He said, and there was light. Simple! God speaks, and everything appears. Not just light, but also dry land, the sun, animals, and so on.

But did you notice that with people He did not speak like that? Not with Adam, nor with Eve. He did not say, "Let there be people." Instead He said, "Let us make man (male and female) in our image" (Genesis 1:26-27). Genesis 2 expands on how God did exactly that: how He made human beings, and in His image. Genesis 2:7 tells us that God formed the first man, Adam, out of the dust of the ground, and breathed into his nostrils the breath of life, and the man became a living being. God actually formed Adam, shaped him, as though he were a sand sculpture by the ocean, and then breathed life into him.

The same is true of Eve. When God saw that Adam was alone, He said, "It is not good for the man to be alone." He did not then say, "Let there be a woman to be a wife for the man!" He said instead, "I will make a helper suitable for him." And then God took a rib from Adam while he slept, and Genesis 2:22 literally says that God built a woman from the rib. He formed the rib into a woman.

Why does God do this? As with everything else, He could have said, "Let there be a man and a woman," and they would have appeared exactly as they are. Why does He take such personal care to shape and form and build them?

It is because human beings are made in God's image. That makes us the crown of His creation, as Psalm 8 also shows. And that means that, unlike any other creature, God wants to have a personal relationship with us. We know this from the first stanza of Psalm 139 (verses 1-6): "O LORD, you have searched me and you know me." When we think of "knowing" someone, as in "Do you know Mike from accounting?" we mean, "Do you know his name and/or recognize his face?" But "knowing" someone in Scripture is much deeper than that. It signifies a very personal, intimate relationship. To "know" someone is to know how they think, what they love. In its most deeply relational, "knowing" is used in Scripture as a euphemism for sexual intercourse. It shows a deep knowledge and personal connection to someone.

God knows us, deeply, intimately, completely. He doesn't just know our name or what we look like, but He fully knows us – He knows our thoughts, He knows what words we will speak before we say them. He knows our desires and our loves. He wants, and He has, a personal, deep connection with His people.

The second stanza of the psalm (verses 7-12) shows how far that care and connection goes: there is absolutely nowhere in this entire universe that we could go where God is not with us and will not find us.

Then the third stanza shows how long that care and connection has been in place: it begins already in the womb, when God takes personal care and attention to shape each one of us. Psalm 139 teaches us that the personal shaping of each individual was not just limited to Adam and Eve. It was true for David too, and so it is true for each of us. Verses 13 and 15 contain two different verbs usually used for clothing manufacturing: weaving and embroidering. Nowadays we have computerized sewing machines for a very hands-off process, but back then clothing was very carefully, individually, and personally woven together. That is the metaphor David uses for growing in his mother's womb – a careful crafting. God is not hands-off. He does not let unborn children grow and see what happens. He personally shapes them into the person He wants them to be.

Isn't that just so wonderful! That shows how much each unborn child means to God. He weaves them together, He embroiders them. Every child is knit together by God. Every child is exactly as God intended her or him to be. Whether she is "healthy" humanly speaking, or he does not live past a few weeks' gestation, every human being is "fearfully and wonderfully made." And so, along with David in verse 14, we praise God for every life. God does not make mistakes. We can delight and take great joy and comfort in the fact that He is personally concerned with each one of us, beginning with how we are made in our mother's womb with intimate care.

And God's care for us doesn't end there – every day of our lives and what is going to happen to us has been ordained by God (verse 16).

So that's what makes human beings so special. It's not really about who we are; rather, it's about who God is and what He has done for us. God is so great, and if we matter so much to Him, if He takes such good care of us, if He personally shapes us, then every life, unborn or born, is sacred.

WHAT MAKES ABORTION SO AWFUL

God, we learn from this psalm, knits each and every human being in their mother's womb. He weaves us together. Abortion, meanwhile, quite literally rips that creation apart and tears it to pieces.

If a child had spent hours painstakingly putting together a wooden castle, and then in one second of meanness his brother came along and kicked it over, we would be very angry. "Why would you do that? Do you have no respect for your brother? Look how much work he put in to that!" That's also why abortion is so awful. It wantonly destroys not just any part of creation, which would be bad enough, but a precious human life which God has knit and woven together. Abortion rightly makes us angry: "Don't you know what that is? Do you have no respect for God's awesome creative power, how much precision and care He put into so carefully forming that child?"

RIGHTEOUS ANGER

After the beautiful words of the first three stanzas of the psalm, the flow seems to be broken up by verse 19. After reflecting on the precious works and thoughts of God, we read, "If only you would slay the wicked, O God!" What a contrast! As we consider the horror of abortion, we wonder what to think of these words. Are we, perhaps, to pray these words about abortionists? How do they fit in with the ethos of the New Testament, about loving your enemies, etc.?

Notice exactly how the psalmist characterizes these men, and how it relates to the rest of the psalm. First of all, these wicked men are bloodthirsty. They have no respect for life. In fact, they destroy that precious life which, as we have seen, God has carefully knit together from conception. They pay no heed to the fact that it is God who ordains and numbers our days – they want to take lives into their own hands. Furthermore, they speak against God with evil intent. They plot against His authority and reject His sovereignty, which has been so beautifully displayed in the first part of the psalm. These men are deliberately rebelling against God.

And don't forget, the wicked themselves are people whom God also knit together fearfully and wonderfully. And yet, instead of praising God, they blaspheme Him. That's what gives David such righteous anger. That mouth you use to blaspheme God, He made it! Those hands you use to murder people God fashioned, He made those! And yet you slander Him. You deliberately reject Him, the one who made you so carefully and awesomely. How dare you!

David has righteous anger against those who reject such an awesome God, their Creator, ignoring everything He has done for them. I read a satirical article titled, "'What Has God Ever Done For Me?' Asks Man Breathing Air." Rejection of God is blind, and ridiculous!

And so, David calls on God to bring justice. But this is no personal vendetta. He very carefully calls down destruction on God's enemies (verse 21) – not those who hate David, but those who hate God. As one who hates evil and loves God, David does not want anything to do with such evil. He hates and abhors wickedness, and wants it destroyed for the sake of God's glory. And David does not contain this zeal against evil only to others, but he even directs it against himself. He welcomes God in verse 23 to search (and reveal) any wickedness in him. Verse 24 contrasts the two ways to live: the "offensive way" and the "way everlasting." David knows the offensive way leads only to destruction, and he seeks God's help to be led in the way everlasting.

Today in Christ we are called not to seek vengeance, but to love and pray for our personal enemies. God will avenge, we are told. So, it's not good for us to pray a prayer such as this against specific people. We don't know people's hearts, and we do not know the future. Loving our enemies means praying for their repentance, recognizing that even though now they are God's enemies, by nature we were all God's enemies. Romans 5:10 reads, "For if, when we were God's enemies, we were reconciled to him through the death of his Son, how much more, having been reconciled, shall we be saved through his life!" The only reason we are not now God's enemies, worthy of death and destruction, is because Christ has saved us. So, we ought to pray for that same undeserved blessing for our unbelieving friends, neighbours and acquaintances – and even our enemies.

On the other hand, we too may be filled with a righteous anger against those who murder the innocent, who with obscene arrogance reject the God who made them. We rightly abhor and hate such wickedness. And so, while we do pray for the salvation of the sinner, we also acknowledge that such rebellion deserves death. Knowing that God is both merciful and just, there is no contradiction between praying on the one hand that He will have mercy, save and lead to repentance even our (personal) enemies, while also praying that

He will bring His righteous judgment and wrath against those who unrepentantly murder the innocent and blaspheme His great and holy name.

And, like David, we acknowledge that we are no better by ourselves. Without God leading us in the way everlasting, we too would be on the offensive way, still enemies of God. Only with His Spirit working in us can we delight in and praise God for His perfections: that He knows everything about us, that He is always with us, that He knit us together so fearfully and wonderfully, and that He is a holy God.

PRAYER POINTS

- Thank God for making you His child, removing your status as His enemy
- Pray for a turning in the hearts of many to follow God, including those who promote and perform abortions, that they might turn and become advocates for life
- Ask God to punish wickedness and defend His glory
- Praise God for His perfection and creative power
- Ask God to search your heart and know you, and reveal to you your deep need for Him

DISCUSSION QUESTIONS

1. Consider the unique process of creation as it applies to human beings. How does it impact you to know that you are something special in God's eyes?

2. Righteous anger is a difficult emotion to get right. How can you keep your anger focused on what angers God, and not allow it to become personal? What gets in the way of doing this?

3. There is an old expression that asks, "Have you prayed about it as much as you've talked about it?" How might this apply to the issues of abortion, euthanasia, or other cultural decay we may see around us?

4. God knits children together in their mother's womb, and He does not make mistakes. How do you balance this truth with experiences of miscarriages, stillbirths, and disabilities? Why do we say these are not mistakes?

5. The blood of Jesus is powerful enough to cover any sin. Do we treat our fellow Christians as though this is true when they publicly repent from sins such as abortion? Can you think of times when someone experienced more guilt from other people than from God? How can we do better at showing Christ's love to sinners within the church community?

PROVERBS 24: 1-12

Be not envious of evil men,
  nor desire to be with them,
for their hearts devise violence,
  and their lips talk of trouble.
By wisdom a house is built,
  and by understanding it is established;
by knowledge the rooms are filled
  with all precious and pleasant riches.
A wise man is full of strength,
  and a man of knowledge enhances his might,
for by wise guidance you can wage your war,
  and in abundance of counselors there is victory.
Wisdom is too high for a fool;
  in the gate he does not open his mouth.
Whoever plans to do evil
  will be called a schemer.
The devising of folly is sin,
  and the scoffer is an abomination to mankind.
If you faint in the day of adversity,
  your strength is small.
Rescue those who are being taken away to death;
  hold back those who are stumbling to the slaughter.
If you say, "Behold, we did not know this,"
  does not he who weighs the heart perceive it?
Does not he who keeps watch over your soul know it,
  and will he not repay man according to his work?

FACING ADVERSITY WITH COURAGE

ABEL C. POL
Victoria, 2016

Suggested song: "IF GOD IS ON OUR SIDE"
Scripture reading: PROVERBS 24:1-12

The phrase "March for Life" has a festive ring to it, doesn't it? A March for Life! It is entirely appropriate for us to participate in this - after all, we serve a God of life. God enjoys endless life. He sent Christ to redeem life, so that we could share in His life. And He gives us the Holy Spirit, the Lord and giver of life. So, for us as Christians to take part in a March for Life is entirely natural. And yet, the reason we do this is actually a sad one. The March for Life would not be necessary if it were not for the presence of abortion in our country. Perhaps that makes some of us nervous, knowing how committed some are to preserving access to abortion here in Canada.

I became involved in pro-life work in my university days, and I encountered a great deal of hostility. It was very intimidating. That same hostility exists today. After all, the position that we maintain is one that abortion advocates despise. And the awareness that we are despised by others is intimidating. It can make us experience fear, which can be paralyzing. It is easier to do a march like this together than to do it on our own.

You could legitimately argue that our main opposition doesn't even come from abortion advocates, but from ourselves. We are held back by our own sense of fear, and perhaps inadequacy. And we are also held back by apathy. Not only our own, but that of those around us. Perhaps you have family members and friends who are not interested in being part of pro-life action. Perhaps you know fellow Christians who believe that abortion is a secular problem, not one that the church should get involved in. And yet our text cuts through all those restrictions and excuses: it tells us clearly that God calls us to stand up.

RESCUE THE VICTIMS

Our text tells us to "rescue those who are being taken away to death; hold back those who are stumbling to the slaughter." Who are those being taken away to death? The text doesn't give us any clues about their identity or circumstances. All it tells us is to "rescue those being taken away to death." That means it applies in many different situations. The one situation it doesn't apply to is the capital punishment of a convicted criminal – the Bible is in favour of capital punishment in certain situations. Romans 13:4, for example, refers to the government bearing the sword. Yet here it tells us to rescue those who are being taken away to death. So, whoever they are who need rescuing from death, they must be legally innocent.

The text doesn't ask us to find out who they are. All it asks us to do is to make sure that the innocent are not killed. And who could possibly be more innocent than the unborn? Who could possibly be more innocent then those who have never had the opportunity to live outside of the womb? Their only crime is that they exist. If we applied that line of reasoning to any other people group – seeing their very existence as a problem to be solved – we would be guilty of the grossest possible form of discrimination. People would be appalled. And yet, we live in a time when abortion is not only tolerated, but defended as a human right.

Since our text doesn't spell out who should be rescued, or what kind of death they should be rescued from, I think we could also argue that it is a call for us to rescue people from choices that lead to death - physical death, but also emotional and spiritual death. That means the victims can also include the women who undergo abortions. It would be wrong of us to focus only on the pre-born human child, and ignore its mother. Yes, there are a huge number of women who voluntarily choose to abort their children. But there are also many women who are pressured into making this choice that will have long-term consequences for them. They too suffer unjustly. It would be wrong for us not to focus on their needs as well. It is easy to speak out against abortion while forgetting that often there are two victims. God calls us to stand up for the innocent, for those who are unjustly oppressed and destroyed, and that is not only the unborn.

A GOD WHO DEFENDS THE WEAK

Why does God call us to stand up for the innocent? Because that is a part of His character. The Bible makes it very clear that God has compassion for the widow, the fatherless, the oppressed. So many of the Old Testament laws refer to caring for these vulnerable groups. Look at psalms such as Psalm 68:5: "A father to the fatherless, a defender of widows, is God in his holy dwelling." Who is more fatherless than the pre-born children whose mothers are pressured into abortion? Who is more oppressed than the pre-born, who are ripped limb from limb in the womb? Who is more defenceless? The pre-born have nothing to fall back on; they are weak, poor, and utterly helpless.

2 Peter 1:4 says that we share in God's divine nature. If you belong to God, you share in His nature - true believers reflect the nature of God. God is a God who has compassion for those who are oppressed. We ought to reflect that compassion as well, both to the pre-born and to their parents. That is part of God's call to stand up for the innocent.

A CALL TO ACTION

Another reason why God calls us to stand up for the innocent is because He will hold us to account if we don't. Look at verse 12 of Proverbs 24: "If you say, 'Behold, we did not know this,' does not he who weighs the heart perceive it? Does not he who keeps watch over your soul know it, and will he not repay man according to his work?" Our passage warns that we will be held to account for the injustice that we ignore – not just in this area of life, but in all areas of life. This is humbling because all of us have engaged in making excuses, and looked the other way when faced with injustice.

All of us live in the presence of the God who weighs our motives and examines our hearts. We cannot plead ignorance. As Christians, we should never want to plead ignorance of injustice. If we share in God's character, we will share in His hatred of injustice. We will want to know what is going on, and we will not want to remain passive. Remaining passive means being indirectly complicit. Going to a March for Life, or other pro-life event, is a way of raising awareness of injustice, simply with our presence. Our presence tells others that our eyes are open to the injustice around us, and we stand for those who cannot stand for themselves. We do this because God calls us to stand up for the innocent.

God calls us to stand up for the innocent - you probably knew that already. But if you have been involved in anything pro-life for a while, you will also know that it can be very intimidating. How can we deal with that? How can we best go about standing up for the innocent when we feel intimidated? Here is where verse 10 of our text speaks to us. It says, "If you faint in the day of adversity, your strength is small." Maybe "faint" is not the best translation. The idea is more one of being discouraged. "If you become discouraged when you face adversity, your strength is small." Adversity here refers to being in a cramped space, in a tight spot. There's actually a pun happening here. You could loosely translate it to say something like, "If you are discouraged in the day of narrowness, how narrow is your strength!"

Now you might think, "That doesn't help me at all. I mean, I get discouraged often. How does this motivate me to break with that discouragement?" But actually, it does. How, you ask? Because it points to the foolishness of letting your courage, your strength, be determined by your circumstances. If your circumstances determine whether or not you feel discouraged, then you'll often be discouraged, because speaking out for the pro-life cause will often put you in a tight spot. There's a reason why verse 10 comes before verse 11. God knows that speaking out for the innocent will mean you encounter opposition. He knows that trying to stand for the oppressed will make you realize that your own strength is small. But, says the text, don't be discouraged by that! Instead, this text invites us to know that our resources are inadequate, and then to find strength by looking beyond ourselves.

HE GIVES EVERYTHING WE NEED

Yes, our resources are inadequate - not only for courage, but for love. God calls us to love our neighbour, also our tiny pre-born neighbours. We don't have that much love in us. Apathy is much easier, and more natural. So, we need to look beyond ourselves to the God of love. The God of love saw that we are loveless people. He reached out to us in Jesus Christ, born as a baby, weak, poor, and utterly helpless. He entered our helplessness to save us from the inside out. He lived and died for sinners like us. All of our lovelessness and apathy and discouragement was nailed to the cross. And He rose again, and He reigns, and He promises to give us abundant strength and courage! "His divine power has given us everything we need for life and godliness through our knowledge of him who called us by his own glory and goodness." (2 Peter 1:3) If we look beyond ourselves to Him, we will experience His encouraging power.

God's way of giving us courage is often to put us in challenging positions. Pro-life work can definitely put you in some challenging positions. But He does that after telling us that He will be with us. God calls us to stand up to injustice, and He invites us to do so with

His strength. Only then will our faith remain strong. Only then can we face the day of adversity with courage. And only then can we stand up in love for the innocent.

PRAYER POINTS

- Pray for a heart that hates injustice, and eyes to see injustice around you
- Thank God for His compassionate heart for the vulnerable, and His love for sinners
- Thank God for a pro-life community, that He allows us to stand together, not alone
- Ask God to give you courage to stand up to adversity in a way that glorifies Him
- Ask God for challenging situations to practice your perseverance and courage. Thank Him for times in your life when you have felt Him carry you through difficult situations
- Pray for an end to the injustice of abortion

DISCUSSION QUESTIONS

1. Do you ever discuss pro-life issues with your friends, or do you just assume most of them are pro-life? How can talking to pro-life friends build our courage and commitment to the cause?

2. Discuss the difference between being legally innocent and biblically innocent.

3. Read Matthew 10:16-33. Re-read verse 28. How can you keep this perspective at the forefront of your mind when you are tempted to stay quiet to avoid being hated or mocked?

4. Do you find it hard to pray for challenging situations in which to practice perseverance and courage? Do you prefer to pray for a peaceful life? Would praying for opportunities to witness change the way you noticed and used those opportunities?

PSALM 27: 7-10 (NIV)

Hear my voice when I call, Lord;
be merciful to me and answer me.
My heart says of you, "Seek his face!"
Your face, Lord, I will seek.
Do not hide your face from me,
do not turn your servant away in anger;
you have been my helper.
Do not reject me or forsake me,
God my Saviour.
Though my father and mother forsake me,
the Lord will receive me.

LOVE THE LITTLE WITH BIG LOVE

BILL DEJONG
Ottawa, 2016

Suggested song: **BEHOLD, THE AMAZING GIFT OF LOVE**
Scripture reading: **PSALM 27: 7-10 (NIV)**

The kingdom of Jesus is for the last, the lost, the least, the languishing, and the little. The kingdom of Jesus is about loving others with big love.

Many of you are no doubt familiar with the name of Mother Teresa. She won a Nobel Peace Prize in 1979, and after winning the prize she delivered the Nobel lecture. In that lecture she said, and I paraphrase: "We must always remember that God loves us and that we have the opportunity to love others the way that God loves us - not in big ways, but in small ways; not in big things, but in small things with great love." For my wife and me, fostering is about loving the little with big love.

I love fostering. I'm going to talk about fostering in relation to the pro-life movement, and I'm going to make my remarks in the context of Psalm 27:7-10:

"Hear my voice when I call, Lord; be merciful to me and answer me. My heart says of you, "Seek his face!" Your face, Lord, I will seek. Do not hide your face from me, do not turn your servant away in anger; you have been my helper. Do not reject me or forsake me, God my Saviour. Though my father and mother forsake me, the Lord will receive me."

The little are vulnerable. It's something we all readily grant when it comes to unborn children – they do not have the capacity to speak, or reason, so they cannot prove their worth, they cannot show their value. But what about the babies that are already born? Little infants also cannot speak, cannot prove their worth, cannot show their value. Yet, the kingdom of Jesus is for the little. Whether born or unborn, these little people have inherent worth as human beings, and they have no need to prove their value to anyone. Abortion cuts short a life, devalued for its littleness and its location. But there are also many little ones who are born, and each one of these children is in need of big love, love like that which we have been shown by our Father. But not all children are born into a place where big love is what welcomes them.

A NEED FOR LOVE

The women whose babies end up in foster care are beautiful women, created in the image of God, having all the dignity that all human beings have, but they have tragic stories. In some cases, they are mentally ill, or mentally disabled, or homeless. In other cases, their lives have been sabotaged by evil, and in some of those cases they have been willing participants, willing accomplices. In most cases they have pain in their lives, and they self-medicate and so become substance abusers, heroin addicts, meth addicts, crack addicts. In some cases, they are HIV-positive. In almost all cases they have no support community. They are estranged even from their own families. These women give birth to children who are in some cases very healthy, and in other cases HIV-positive, or crying inconsolably, shaking, wailing, clenching their muscles because they're going through the symptoms of withdrawal from heroin addiction.

Perhaps you can hear the protest of people. How irresponsible of these women! Unfit to be mothers! Why did they choose to keep their babies? Why didn't they terminate the pregnancies? Who's going to care for their children, since they are obviously so ill-equipped to care for them themselves?

My wife and I, and many people in the fostering and adoption network, have said, It's true. They are irresponsible. They are probably unfit to be mothers. BUT, we are so, so happy they decided to keep their babies, and did not terminate their pregnancy. We will care for those babies. God has loved us with an endless, abundant love, and we want to love others with the love with which God has loved us. We want to love the little with big love.

AUTHENTIC, SACRIFICIAL LOVE

My wife tells me that too often, when I talk about fostering, I romanticize the vocation, and that I need to bridle my enthusiasm with realism, because there are challenges that are associated with fostering. But, I hope you consider the vocation of fostering or adoption for your own life, now or maybe in the future, and if not, at least I hope you will see it as an important role that people must play in the pro-life movement.

What are the challenges of fostering? The challenges all have to do with sacrifices that you have to make. You have to sacrifice sleep, especially if you have newborns, particularly if you have newborn twins, as we did recently. And if you're going to lose sleep, you have to be prepared to lose your sanity. You have to be prepared to sacrifice space in your home, because foster children need their own bedrooms, and plenty of room to enjoy their toys. You have to be prepared to sacrifice your freedom: you can't go where you want, do what you want, when you want – you have a baby to care for. There are bottles to prepare, diapers to change, medications to administer. There will be plenty of times when your friends want to go out and do something and you have to say no because of your responsibilities to a child.

But most importantly, you have to be prepared to sacrifice your heart. People will say, "I could never be a foster parent, I love children too much, I could never say goodbye." But actually, that tenderness of heart is exactly what qualifies you to be a foster parent! We want foster parents to love their foster children with precisely that depth of love.

A moment will come when the foster baby will go back to his mother, or she may go to an adoptive family. And your heart will literally break, and you will cry to the point that your tear ducts will literally be empty of tears. You will walk into the bedroom of the child you had in your home for one year, two years, the child that you cared for from the moment she was born, and you will see only an empty bed, maybe some toys sitting there. If your heart isn't broken by this, you're not fit to be a foster parent. You are to give foster children authentic, parental love. If you are not a mess when they leave, you shouldn't be a foster parent.

We do not know how many days we will be given with our biological children – there are no guarantees, and there is definitely a possibility of devastating heartbreak. This does not prevent us from having children, or from loving them with our whole hearts. All children that come into our care are ultimately in God's hand, and ours to parent only for as long as He gives us.

We must love the little with big love. There is much sacrifice required to love with the love with which God loves us. But God could not have given us a clearer example of sacrifice to follow than that of His Son Jesus Christ, who died on the cross in our place. Christianity comes with sacrifice. Nowhere does Jesus say it will be easy. You have to be prepared to sacrifice much, including your heart.

TO LOVE AND BE LOVED

Let me conclude with some of the joys of fostering. My wife and I have only had newborns, so I speak from limited experience. But fostering introduces you – or re-introduces you! – to the joy of babies. We live in a highly competitive world where people are always assessing us, always judging us, but these little babies always love you, always delight in you, are thrilled to see you just the way you are.

My wife and I have teenagers – it's been a while since we had babies. We can enjoy again everything that a baby offers – the giggles of baby joy, playing peekaboo, singing lullabies. Foster babies unite families – they have an incredible power to bring a family together. We are a foster family, which means that everyone in our family, including our teenage boys, plays a part. They all change diapers, heat up bottles, and do laundry. Foster babies can subdue selfishness. It is so rewarding for me to see one of my teenage boys put his iPod away, or press pause on the PlayStation, to help a cranky baby simply because he wants to, because he loves her.

Babies are powerful: they can transform you. Though they have no strength, they can captivate your heart. Though they cannot speak, you listen to them attentively. Though they cannot understand, you speak to them deliberately. Though they are uneducated, they teach you that human dignity does not lie in saying things, or thinking things, or doing things, but simply in being someone. Human value does not lie in saying, thinking, or doing, but simply in being someone created in the image of God, to love and to be loved.

The kingdom of Jesus is for the last, the lost, the least, the languishing, and the little. It's for those whom the world pushes aside, judges to be a burden, wishes to dispose of as unwanted, or regards as subhuman. Jesus says, "You are precious. I love you, and I want you in my kingdom."

What a kingdom we are blessed to be a part of – a kingdom of big love, sacrificial love, love that has no basis in our abilities, achievements, or assets. We must remember how richly God loves us, and use the opportunities He gives to love others in the same way. Love the little with big love.

PRAYER POINTS

- Give thanks for God's big, sacrificial love for you
- Give thanks that our value and dignity are not based on what we say, think or do, and ask God to help you find your identity in Him
- Pray for families who are fostering, or thinking about becoming foster parents
- Pray for clarity in your life, if fostering or adoption is something God would have you do
- Pray for birth mothers, that they may find peace and wholeness in Jesus
- Pray for children in foster care, that they may be loved in a way that teaches them their God-given value
- Pray for those who work in child services and are a first contact for children and families in crisis

DISCUSSION QUESTIONS

1. Read 1 John 3:1-3, Galatians 4:1-7 and Ephesians 1:3-14. Reflect on your adoption as a child of God, a fellow heir with Christ. How does this truth impact your view of earthly fostering and adoption?

2. What are some things that you feel would hold you back from fostering or adopting? If you are involved in fostering/adopting, how would you encourage others considering doing the same?

3. How can you support foster families in your church community? How you can support pro-life efforts in your broader community?

4. How can our valuing of children and family reflect God's love for the last, the lost, the least, the languishing and the little among and around us?

5. What are ways besides fostering and adoption that we can love as God loves, and show great love in small things?

JUDGES 6:1-16 (KJV)

And the children of Israel did evil in the sight of the Lord: and the Lord delivered them into the hand of Midian seven years.

And the hand of Midian prevailed against Israel: and because of the Midianites the children of Israel made them the dens which are in the mountains, and caves, and strong holds.

And so it was, when Israel had sown, that the Midianites came up, and the Amalekites, and the children of the east, even they came up against them;

And they encamped against them, and destroyed the increase of the earth, till thou come unto Gaza, and left no sustenance for Israel, neither sheep, nor ox, nor ass.

For they came up with their cattle and their tents, and they came as grasshoppers for multitude; for both they and their camels were without number: and they entered into the land to destroy it.

And Israel was greatly impoverished because of the Midianites; and the children of Israel cried unto the Lord.

And it came to pass, when the children of Israel cried unto the Lord because of the Midianites,

That the Lord sent a prophet unto the children of Israel, which said unto them, Thus saith the Lord God of Israel, I brought you up from Egypt, and brought you forth out of the house of bondage;

And I delivered you out of the hand of the Egyptians, and out of the hand of all that oppressed you, and drave them out from before you, and gave you their land;

And I said unto you, I am the Lord your God; fear not the gods of the Amorites, in whose land ye dwell: but ye have not obeyed my voice.

And there came an angel of the Lord, and sat under an oak which was in Ophrah, that pertained unto Joash the Abiezrite: and his son Gideon threshed wheat by the winepress, to hide it from the Midianites.

And the angel of the Lord appeared unto him, and said unto him, The Lord is with thee, thou mighty man of valour.

And Gideon said unto him, Oh my Lord, if the Lord be with us, why then is all this befallen us? and where be all his miracles which our fathers told us of, saying, Did not the Lord bring us up from Egypt? but now the Lord hath forsaken us, and delivered us into the hands of the Midianites.

And the Lord looked upon him, and said, Go in this thy might, and thou shalt save Israel from the hand of the Midianites: have not I sent thee?

And he said unto him, Oh my Lord, wherewith shall I save Israel? behold, my family is poor in Manasseh, and I am the least in my father's house.

And the Lord said unto him, Surely I will be with thee, and thou shalt smite the Midianites as one man.

GOD USES THE WEAK

DAVID LIPSY
Ottawa, 2016

Suggested song: **PSALM 121**
Scripture reading: **JUDGES 6:1-16**

Our theme is "God uses the weak." You might not feel very encouraged by such a title, but we ought to be! In 1 Cor. 1:26-29 we read the well-known words,

"For ye see your calling, brethren, how that not many wise men after the flesh, not many mighty, not many noble, are called: But God hath chosen the foolish things of the world to confound the wise; and God hath chosen the weak things of the world to confound the things which are mighty; And base things of the world, and things which are despised, hath God chosen, yea, and things which are not, to bring to nought things that are: That no flesh should glory in his presence." (KJV)

That passage has been encouraging to me personally, for I often feel myself to be very weak.

The history we read in Judges 6 is honest, disappointing, and frustrating in parts, and yet, if rightly considered, it can be very, very encouraging. Let's consider the historical context. As they had so often done before, Israel once again turned from serving the Lord. God used the Midianites as His instrument of chastening, for seven long years. Theirs was a particularly severe dominance, as one of Midian's methods of affliction was to destroy Israel's food. It took a while, but eventually, in desperation, Israel cried to the Lord for help.

Instead of sending a deliverer right away, God sends a prophet (verse 8). The prophet's message was not particularly encouraging. Through the prophet, God proclaimed that He was Israel's God, the one who brought them out of bondage once before. He drove out all opposition in Canaan and gave them the land. He had told them not to worship other gods, but they did not obey Him. That was it. End of message.

Think about the time we're living in and what is happening in our nation. Are we crying out to the Lord with a sense of urgency? If we are, God would be just to send us the same message – you have turned from Me! I told you how to live, and you failed to listen.

Though this initial response seems to be more like a deaf ear than a helping hand, God did then appear in visible form as the "angel of the Lord." But He did not appear to the elders of Israel, or send them a prominent leader. Instead, God appeared to Gideon, who said of himself, "Behold, my family is poor in Manasseh, and I am the least in my father's house" (verse 15). We don't know how old Gideon was, but he was still living at home at the time of God's first appearance to him.

GOD'S MESSAGE

What did God say to Gideon? "The LORD is with thee, thou mighty man of valour" (verse 12). This was a fascinating beginning. God didn't first address Israel's troubles, or His plans for Gideon. Instead, He began by saying I AM JEHOVAH. Then He added a promise: "I am with you." Then He described Gideon as a "mighty man of valour."

God's message to Gideon seems a bit off key at first glance. Didn't God know that Gideon would be afraid, try to avoid taking action, ask for signs, etc.? Yes, God knew it. But God was simply saying to Gideon what He would say to Paul centuries later, and what He says to us today, "My grace is sufficient for thee: for my strength is made perfect in weakness." (2 Corinthians 12:9, KJV) These words of God to Gideon and to Paul should be a mighty encouragement to us too as we look to defend pre-born children.

Are we not weak? Outnumbered? Outgunned politically? You might have asked yourself, "What can I possibly do when the problems in our nation seem insurmountable?" We need to remember that "The LORD is with you" is the single most important matter in our entire life – personally, as churches, and as a pro-life movement.

GIDEON'S RESPONSE

Gideon was not so quickly persuaded. "And Gideon said unto him, Oh my Lord, if the Lord be with us, why then is all this befallen us? and where be all his miracles which our fathers told us of, saying, Did not the Lord bring us up from Egypt? but now the Lord hath forsaken us, and delivered us into the hands of the Midianites" (verse 13). Notice that Gideon actually changed God's Words slightly. God had said, "the LORD is with you" (singular). Gideon said, "If the LORD be with us..." Gideon was judging the Lord's promise by the present circumstances. Why are we, Israel, chastened? Where are God's miracles as with the deliverance from Egypt? The LORD has forsaken us and delivered us to the Midianites.

But something is missing in his reply. Gideon shows no sense of guilt. Gideon should have confessed something like, "Of course the chastisements of the Lord are upon Israel, for we have sinned!" But Gideon didn't repent over Israel's sins, or even his own sins. Instead, he just lamented the consequences. By contrast, Daniel was very different (see Daniel 9). His prayers of repentance for Israel included himself. He owned Israel's sin and pleaded God's covenant mercies.

Aren't we part of Canada's problems? Can we actually expect the world to identify and repent over our sins as a nation? Do we expect deliverance from our wickedness to be ushered in by our political leaders? Who but we the church can be expected to be the intercessors and agents of change whom God uses for good? May God give us the grace to start there ourselves, in humble confession.

GOD SPEAKS AGAIN

In verse 14 we read, "And the LORD looked upon him, and said, 'Go in this thy might, and thou shalt save Israel from the hand of the Midianites; have I not sent thee?'" Instead of debating with Gideon, God sends the man to take on the very task Gideon complained was not getting done: "...save Israel from the hand of the Midianites: have not I sent thee?" That's the message for you today. God is sending you. He is sending me. Don't look at someone else or some organization. He's addressing us! God wills to use the weak.

Gideon is stuck. Why? Because he looks at himself! "Please, Lord, how can I save Israel? Behold, my clan is the weakest in Manasseh, and I am the least in my father's house." It's as though Gideon was asking, "How could I ever do what you're asking me to do?" But God never said Gideon had to do anything himself. Remember, "The LORD is with you" and "I have sent you"? That too is the message for you today. God says to us as His people, "This is My fight. We will labour together in this cause!"

God looked upon Gideon. I have to wonder how many times the Lord looks upon us. "Will he, will she, never learn? It is not by human might, not by human power, but by My Spirit. I do not need your strength. I will instead use your weakness so as to display My strength. Your strength and gifts and accomplishments would bring you glory. I do all these things through your weakness so that it brings Me glory!"

One of our biggest problems is the same as Gideon's. We honestly don't like to be weak. We need God's grace to really want all the glory to go to the Lord. It's easy to say, "to God be the glory," but is that really, really what we desire?

GOD'S PATIENT INSTRUCTION

Gideon looked at himself and thought, "There's no way I can do this." How did God answer that? How does He still answer such thoughts? By building Gideon up? By showing Gideon all his wonderful personal qualities that will well-equip him for the task he's being given? Not quite. Verse 16 reads, "And the Lord said unto him, 'Surely I will be with thee, and thou shalt smite the Midianites as one man.'"

I will be with you. You shall strike them all as one man. There is certainty and promise, alongside the call to trust. The bottom line for Gideon, and for us, is whether we actually believe what God says, and what He has revealed to us through His Word. Is the Lord enough for us? His Word, His promises, His warnings?

It was the same story when Israel refused to trust that God could bring them into the land of Canaan the first time. God's response then was, "How long will this people provoke me? and how long will it be ere they believe me, for all the signs which I have shewed among them?" (Numbers 14:11, KJV) Think of what the Lord said to Pharaoh in his obstinacy: "How long wilt thou refuse to humble thyself before me?" (Exodus 10:3, KJV) This is actually what is behind our unbelief...it is pride.

For Gideon, and for us, God is patient but firm with human weakness and doubt. Three signs later, Gideon has gained confidence in God's strength and – with a whittled-down army and a seemingly ridiculous battle plan – total victory! When we listen to God, look for evidence of His power, and trust in His might, we may expect the same!

GOD'S MESSAGE TO US TODAY

There's a passage in Proverbs that is calling out to us in our time. "If thou forbear to deliver them that are drawn unto death, and those that are ready to be slain; If thou sayest, Behold, we knew it not; doth not he that pondereth the heart consider it? and he that keepeth thy soul, doth not he know it? and shall not he render to every man according to his works?" (Prov. 24:11-12, KJV).

It is so gratifying to see so many Christians involved in pro-life action. Like Gideon, we are called to get involved, and to trust God with the results. If you ask, "What can I do?" the answer is "Plenty!" ARPA Canada and We Need a LAW, the Canadian Centre for Bioethical Reform (CCBR), Cardus, Campaign Life Coalition, local Right to Life chapters, pregnancy care centres, Safe Families Canada, and local church-related efforts are all open doors of opportunity for you, friends. They all need some sweat equity. If you can't do, then give! Find a way to be involved and stay involved!

But let's never forget the lesson learned from Gideon. The power is not in us. It is only in God's Word and His Spirit! It was so with Gideon. It was so with the apostle Paul. It is so with us today. We thank God for using us in our weakness and take confidence in the declaration of our living, reigning Saviour, "All power is given unto me in heaven and in earth" (Matthew 28:18). Go in this, His might!

PRAYER POINTS

- Thank God for choosing to work through weakness, and ask Him to use you in His kingdom work
- Ask for forgiveness from pride and glory-seeking, and ask for the Spirit to give you a desire to bring glory to God in all you do
- Pray for God to bring Himself glory through organizations that are working daily to bring God's truth to the public square
- Read Daniel's prayer in Daniel 9 and confess your sin and our nation's sin in a similar way

DISCUSSION QUESTIONS

1. Think of other examples of people in the Bible where we see God use human weakness to accomplish His purposes. How is this encouraging to us as followers of Christ?

2. Read Exodus 2:23 – 4:17 and Isaiah 6. Compare and contrast Gideon's call and response with the call and response of Moses and Isaiah.

3. Read 2 Corinthians 12:9. What is an area in your life where you feel ill equipped for the task God has called you to? Think of a time when getting out of your comfort zone forced you to rely more on God.

4. Do you think we ever fully do things for God's glory and not our own?

5. How can we compliment and encourage others without contributing to pride? How can we give glory to God when expressing appreciation or admiration for someone?

MARK 5:1-15

They came to the other side of the sea, to the country of the Gerasenes. And when Jesus had stepped out of the boat, immediately there met him out of the tombs a man with an unclean spirit. He lived among the tombs. And no one could bind him anymore, not even with a chain, for he had often been bound with shackles and chains, but he wrenched the chains apart, and he broke the shackles in pieces. No one had the strength to subdue him. Night and day among the tombs and on the mountains he was always crying out and cutting himself with stones. And when he saw Jesus from afar, he ran and fell down before him. And crying out with a loud voice, he said, "What have you to do with me, Jesus, Son of the Most High God? I adjure you by God, do not torment me." For he was saying to him, "Come out of the man, you unclean spirit!" And Jesus asked him, "What is your name?" He replied, "My name is Legion, for we are many." And he begged him earnestly not to send them out of the country. Now a great herd of pigs was feeding there on the hillside, and they begged him, saying, "Send us to the pigs; let us enter them." So he gave them permission. And the unclean spirits came out and entered the pigs; and the herd, numbering about two thousand, rushed down the steep bank into the sea and drowned in the sea.

The herdsmen fled and told it in the city and in the country. And people came to see what it was that had happened. And they came to Jesus and saw the demon-possessed man, the one who had had the legion, sitting there, clothed and in his right mind, and they were afraid.

JESUS BRINGS LIFE IN THE MIDST OF DEATH

PETER H. HOLTVLÜWER
Ottawa, 2015

Suggested song: "O FOR A THOUSAND TONGUES TO SING"
Scripture reading: MARK 5:1-15

It doesn't take much to see that our Canadian culture—like the rest of the Western world—is cozying up to death more and more. Putting it that way sounds like an oxymoron—how could anyone become "cozy" with death? And yet since the abortion law was struck down in 1988, Canadians have had unhindered access to the killing of babies within the womb. 100,000 pre-born children are murdered each year and many are comfortable with it. They want it, they like it—that's pretty cozy.

In 2015, our Supreme Court struck down the law against assisted suicide. This is about life on the other end of the spectrum. When someone who is suffering and is able to speak for themselves wants to die, our law now says that such people should not only be allowed to die, but actually helped to die. The court seems to be reflecting some measure of public opinion: if we want to die badly enough, we should be helped to die in as humane a way as possible—that's definitely getting pretty cozy with death. When once death was disdained, even feared, and life was treasured, now death is sought out as an escape, as life is no longer considered a gift from God to be valued and protected.

How strange and contradictory this is to the way of our Saviour Jesus Christ. He came to save life, not destroy it. He came to bring life even in the midst of death, a message that is shown so clearly in Mark 5.

A TORTURED LOVE FOR DEATH

Jesus and his disciples no sooner cross the Sea of Galilee than they are met by a man "with an unclean spirit." A demon. From other parts of the Bible we know that demons are fallen angels who serve Satan—they are his soldiers. Mark tells us three times, so we don't miss it, that this demon-possessed man lived among the tombs—he felt at home in the cemetery, "cozy" among the dead. Luke's Gospel also tells us that this man was naked.

What we have in this man is a picture of Satan's work and goal. God, you remember, created man holy and happy in a garden paradise where he lived naked and without shame. Satan here is doing everything he can to break down God's good creation. This possessed man is filled with sin and shame, living in misery in a graveyard. Filled with a legion of demons—that's more than 6000 evil spirits—this man is one of Satan's greatest projects and playthings, one of his biggest triumphs. The devil is "into" death and loves to have his minions hanging around the tombs. Later, the legion of demons gets sent into a large herd of pigs and instantly drowns 2000 of them—more death.

This devil-controlled man can rip off chains as if they were cobwebs. He is free to do whatever he wants, go wherever he wants, but what he likes is death, what he wants is destruction. Even of himself. Maybe you noticed that as you read verse 5: "Night and day among the tombs and on the mountains he was always crying out and cutting himself with stones." Cutting himself. Crying out in desperation. He has a tortured love for pain and death. Do you see, my friends, how Satan loves to enslave, how life under Satan's influence leads to sorrow, desperation and a longing for death itself? The enemy of God takes away hope and light, and leaves people in despair and darkness, thinking there is nothing better than to put an end to life.

What Satan did to that one man he is now doing to our whole culture. Babies are delivered over to death and it's brushed away as just a bunch of non-human cells. Or, more subtly, a non-person. More and more, suffering adults are not encouraged or helped to keep on living, but they are pointed to a "soft" death as an option, offered assistance to die. They are not given support to overcome or manage frailties, but they are given tools to plunge into death itself. Our own Canadian citizens are so blinded by the evil one that they fight for their right to kill their own children! They can't see how ludicrous that is, let alone how unjust.

A TOTAL LOVE FOR LIFE

Now look at our Saviour. We read in Mark 4:35 that it was His idea to get into the boat and cross the sea—He had an appointment with this demoniac, only the demoniac didn't know it. The Lord went out of His way to touch the life of this miserable, enslaved man—and what does Jesus do? He releases the man from slavery. He bursts through his perma-darkness with the light of His healing power and commands the demon to "Come out of the man!" (verse 8).

6000 demons, who could not be contained or controlled by any man, or even by chains, are easily controlled by the Lord Jesus—Out! Out you go, and never come back! That's what Christ does! Jesus came to earth to take off the chains of the devil and destroy his work. He came to bring life in the midst of a world full of death.

Did you notice how the life and the condition of this former demoniac changed? A crowd from the nearby village came out, and they saw this ex-crazy man at the feet of Jesus, "sitting there, clothed and in his right mind." He was sitting, not running around the mountainside crying and cutting. He was clothed and respectable, not naked and ashamed. He was in his right mind—not blinded or led by the devil any longer, but guided by the Creator and Saviour of the world.

This is a picture of Jesus' work and goal. He has a total love for life, and works to restore human beings to a noble and dignified life—the same way the Lord created us in the beginning. Christ loves life so much that He willingly gave Himself up to death on a cross to secure for His people that right, that privilege. He suffered the full penalty that we incurred for our rebellion against God so that we could be transformed into sons and daughters of God, restored to life in His family.

And if Jesus could do that for you and me, then now as the Ascended King on high in heaven He can surely do it as well for our fellow Canadians! If we meet people who are hateful toward God and life, people who are blind to the culture of death, people who are angry at us for promoting life—remember the power of the Saviour to expel a legion of demons. Remember His mercy in tracking down one enslaved demoniac across the sea. Remember the grace of King Jesus in changing you and me. "I once was lost but now am found. I once was blind, but now I see." In the words of the hymn O For a Thousand Tongues to Sing, "He breaks the power of reigning sin, He sets the prisoners free; His blood can make the foulest clean; His blood avails for me."

PRAYER POINTS

- Praise God for His power over evil and over death
- Praise God for the good gift of life, and for seeking you out to be His child
- Praise God for His transformative work in your life, and the lives of all believers
- Pray for those who are blind to the devil's power in their lives, that their eyes might be opened and more people may praise and glorify God
- Pray for Christ's return, and for full rest in Him

DISCUSSION QUESTIONS

1. Read Ephesians 6:12. How do you feel about this reality? Does viewing the world this way make you more compassionate and gracious in responding to hate from the world?

2. How can we live out our love for life and support those who might be considering abortion or euthanasia? How can we better support the elderly in our community so they don't feel like a burden or lose hope?

3. In abortion we speak for those who cannot speak for themselves. In euthanasia, we speak against those who are speaking for themselves and their right to die. In what way should we then address the two issues differently?

PSALM 72:1-19

Give the king your justice, O God,
  and your righteousness to the royal son!
May he judge your people with righteousness,
  and your poor with justice!
Let the mountains bear prosperity for the people,
  and the hills, in righteousness!
May he defend the cause of the poor of the people,
  give deliverance to the children of the needy, and crush
  the oppressor!
May they fear you while the sun endures,
  and as long as the moon, throughout all generations!
May he be like rain that falls on the mown grass,
  like showers that water the earth!
In his days may the righteous flourish,
  and peace abound, till the moon be no more!
May he have dominion from sea to sea,
  and from the River to the ends of the earth!
May desert tribes bow down before him,
  and his enemies lick the dust!
May the kings of Tarshish and of the coastlands
  render him tribute;
may the kings of Sheba and Seba bring gifts!

May all kings fall down before him,
  all nations serve him!
For he delivers the needy when he calls,
  the poor and him who has no helper.
He has pity on the weak and the needy,
  and saves the lives of the needy.
From oppression and violence he redeems their life,
  and precious is their blood in his sight.
Long may he live;
  may gold of Sheba be given to him!
May prayer be made for him continually,
  and blessings invoked for him all the day!
May there be abundance of grain in the land;
  on the tops of the mountains may it wave;
  may its fruit be like Lebanon;
and may people blossom in the cities
  like the grass of the field!
May his name endure forever,
  his fame continue as long as the sun!
May people be blessed in him,
  all nations call him blessed!
Blessed be the Lord, the God of Israel,
  who alone does wondrous things.
Blessed be his glorious name forever;
  may the whole earth be filled with his glory!
Amen and Amen!

WHERE THERE IS NO VISION, THE PEOPLE PERISH

GEORGE VAN POPTA
Ottawa, 2013

Suggested song: **PSALM 72**
Scripture reading: **PSALM 72:1-19**

Throughout history, humans have violently eliminated large segments of the population through horrific atrocities. For example, the Holocaust in the middle of the 20th century saw the brutal extermination of millions of Jewish people, as well as Gypsies, religious dissenters, and others because of religious and racial prejudice. In every generation there is evidence of man's inhumanity toward man.

Rabbi Yehuda Levin of New York said, "Each form of genocide, whether Holocaust, lynching, or abortion, differs from all the others in the motives and methods of its perpetrators. But each form of genocide is identical to all the others in that it involves the systematic slaughter, as state-sanctioned choice, of innocent, defenceless victims—while denying their personhood."

In Canada, at this time in history, a serious attack on a part of human society continues to take place. Babies in the womb are being killed without regard, by a society that denies them their personhood. What kind of society ends the lives of its unborn children with such disregard? Babies are dying because they are inconvenient, or the "wrong" sex, or less than perfect, or too costly... and they are given no protection by our laws. Three hundred children die each day through abortion. Canada wants to be a just society. But how can a just and civilized society tolerate such a travesty as the wholesale elimination of millions of unborn children?

CHRIST'S KINGSHIP

It is a painful thing that Canada allows this injustice to carry on. It is especially painful when we consider where our nation came from, for many of Canada's founders acknowledged the kingship of Christ over Canada—Christ, who certainly does not approve of the injustice, the crime, of abortion. On Parliament Hill, inscribed above the windows on the Peace Tower, are three Scripture texts! The words carved there into stone prove that the founders of our nation acknowledged the kingship of Christ.

Two of the texts engraved in the stone of the Peace Tower are from Psalm 72: "Give the King thy judgments, O God, and thy righteousness unto the King's son" (verse 1), and "He shall have dominion from sea to sea" (verse 8).

Psalm 72 was meant as a prayer for the reigning king of Israel. This psalm, however, speaks of the king in terms that no mere human leader could attain. It speaks of a king who reigns forever and who rules over all nations. Both Jews and Christians have always understood that, ultimately, Psalm 72 is speaking about the Messiah. It speaks about the King of kings and Lord of lords.

Applying Psalm 72 to our Canadian context, Christ is the one who has dominion from the Atlantic Ocean in the east to the Pacific Ocean in the west to the Arctic Ocean in the north. Every Canadian owes allegiance to King Jesus. These words spoke powerfully to the fathers of the Dominion of Canada. These words of Psalm 72 are also incorporated in the motto on Canada's Coat of Arms: *A mari usque ad mare* (also "from sea to sea").

Psalm 72 speaks of a king who rules in a righteous and merciful way. That's King Jesus, and His standard should be what earthly leaders strive for—and what a standard! Righteous and merciful, majestic, judging without partiality, compassionate, delivering those who call upon Him, having pity on the weak and needy. Many kings and rulers impose heavy burdens upon their citizens. But King Jesus says: Come to me, all you who are weary and burdened, and I will give you rest. ...For my yoke is easy and my burden is light (Matthew 11:28-29).

The kingship of Christ is characterized by righteousness, compassion, justice, mercy, and rest. These attributes are all beautiful things. The trouble with our country is that the leaders and citizens are rejecting the kingship of Christ. There is very little acknowledgment of Him as the king over all of life. They have rejected His words and His revelation, both the gospel and the law.

On Ascension Day, which the Christian church commemorates annually, the church celebrates the ascension of her Lord Jesus Christ to heaven, to the right hand of God. Christ died, rose again, but then also ascended to heaven. There He reigns as king, and from there He will come to judge the living and the dead. Christ is the king spoken of in Psalm 72. He holds justice and righteousness in His hands. He looks from His throne in heaven and sees the injustice perpetrated upon (as Psalm 72 says) the afflicted, the oppressed, the weak. He sees the violence and the bloodshed. It grieves Him to see that happen in a country like Canada, which once thought so highly of Him as to engrave Scripture texts pointing to Him on the Peace Tower.

LACK OF VISION

There is a third text inscribed in the stone of the Peace Tower: "Where there is no vision, the people perish." This vision referred to in Proverbs 29:18 is the revelation of the Word of God. Without the Word of God, people perish. It can also be translated: Where there is no revelation, the people cast off restraint. The Word of God restrains people. It holds us back from sin and foolishness. When people reject the Word of God, rejecting the sovereign and gracious kingship of Christ, they cast off restraint. Rejecting the royal word of Christ the King leads to anarchy and chaos, days like those of the judges where everyone did what was right in his own eyes.

That's what you increasingly see around you. Chaos in the lives of Canadians—individually and nationally. They have largely rejected the King who rules from sea to sea. Our nation has traded the Prince of Peace for King Selfishness and Queen Pleasure. Canadians have lost the vision. They have let go of the revelation of God. They are running wild. And, sadly, the leadership of our country has often led the charge. Think only of Parliament's inaction to enact any kind of abortion law. We have had no law since 1988. For 25 years it has been open season in Canada on the unborn. The King's word has been rejected. The King has been rejected. Restraint has been cast off, and little people perish.

LOOKING FORWARD

But there is a King in heaven: our Lord Jesus Christ, seated at the right hand of God the Father. He sees the crimes being perpetrated against the little ones. He will come again to right every wrong and to establish justice and righteousness upon the earth. In the meantime, as people who believe in Him, and as citizens of this country, we have a task and responsibility to speak up for the rights of Christ the king, and in defence of the weak. It is also our responsibility to pray for the leadership of this country, that the Holy Spirit would give our civic leaders the courage to stand up for truth, justice and righteousness for the little ones—for the unborn.

Let us go forward each day with our eyes fixed on Christ, standing for righteousness, standing for the unborn, for the little boys and the little girls who perish when the people cast off restraint.

PRAYER POINTS

- Thank God for Canada's Christian roots, which impacted so many of our laws and gave us so many of the freedoms we enjoy today
- Pray that our government would again recognize the kingship of Christ and rule as His servants
- Confess your tendency toward selfishness and pleasure-seeking that is no different from the world, and ask God to help you to see areas in your life that need refocusing on Him
- Ask for courage to speak God's Word and revelation in an increasingly hostile culture
- Thank Jesus for dwelling in heaven as our advocate and intercessor, and pray for the gathering of His kingdom so that He can come again and set all things right
- Pray for an awakening in Canada to the wrong of abortion and an end to abortion in Canada

DISCUSSION QUESTIONS

1. Where can you see evidence of Christian roots in Canadian culture and laws today?

2. Where do you see chaos and unhappiness in the lives of Canadians today? How much has the church been impacted by this?

3. Do you find it hard to pray for an end to abortion? Do you believe it is a prayer that pleases God and that He can answer?

4. How do you hold on to the revelation that Christ is King in a society focused on selfishness and pleasure? What are ways we can show that we are different from the world?

PROVERBS 31:1-9

The words of King Lemuel. An oracle that his mother taught him:
What are you doing, my son? What are you doing, son of my womb?
What are you doing, son of my vows?
Do not give your strength to women,
your ways to those who destroy kings.
It is not for kings, O Lemuel,
it is not for kings to drink wine,
or for rulers to take strong drink,
lest they drink and forget what has been decreed
and pervert the rights of all the afflicted.
Give strong drink to the one who is perishing,
and wine to those in bitter distress;
let them drink and forget their poverty
and remember their misery no more.
Open your mouth for the mute,
for the rights of all who are destitute.
Open your mouth, judge righteously,
defend the rights of the poor and needy.

SPEAK FOR THOSE WHO CANNOT SPEAK FOR THEMSELVES

JOHN VAN POPTA

Ottawa, 2012

Suggested song: **PSALM 94**
Scripture reading: **PROVERBS 31:1-9**

Friends, there is a series of lies perpetrated in the media that permeates our culture. It says that the matter of abortion is settled, and that the law of the land cannot be changed. It says that abortion is strictly a private matter, which concerns only a woman and her doctor. But the protection of life goes beyond simply a private matter – it is a matter of public interest.

The problem is, there is no law to restrict abortion in Canada. The law as it stood was struck down by the Supreme Court of

Canada a long time ago. When the court did that, it believed that the government would step in and rewrite the law in a way that it would withstand a constitutional challenge. But no government has done so. The lie continues. The present government refuses to even consider a discussion. The topic is considered "toxic."

It is a cause for sorrow that so much of the Christian community in this country has little interest in social justice. There is a place – and a calling – for the people of God to speak up.

There are also Members of Parliament, across party lines, who believe that some sort of legislation should be in place. When we as citizens stand up for life, we encourage and motivate MPs with the knowledge that there are tens of thousands, even millions, of ordinary citizens in this country who know it is a travesty that harp seals have more rights than pre-born children.

JUSTICE TO THE POOR

The Bible, of course, doesn't foresee widespread aborting of babies, but it speaks of justice to the poor. The poor are those people without means or citizenship. The poor are those afflicted with poverty, or those who were strangers, sojourners, and aliens. The sojourner was the person not of Israel, who lived among the people of God. God, through Moses, commanded the people to defend them, reminding them that in Egypt that was their status – they were the ones who were sojourners. Their own previous status was to be their motivation for social justice. God says, "Take care of those who cannot speak for themselves; take care of the widow, the orphan, the sojourner. Take care of the poor."

The poor are those people without means and without citizenship. Who qualifies more than babies denied personhood?

One of the first steps in the "psychology of oppression" is to deny personhood to someone. Think of times of war. Italians in WW2 were Wops; the Japanese Japs. Germans were Krauts. The Germans in turn considered Jews to be subhuman vermin. So also today, the unborn are not persons, but "products of conception," just "biomass," or even "parasites." Their dead bodies are not corpses, but "bio-medical waste."

The church is called upon to speak for those who cannot speak for themselves. Think of Jesus' inaugural sermon, where He quotes Isaiah: "I've come to preach good news to the poor, liberty for captives" (Isaiah 61:1; Luke 4:18). The Scriptures often direct our attention to the poor, and the poor are not only those who are poor in possessions. I want to encourage you today to think about the poor, and about how we are to consider them.

WHO ARE THE POOR?

You can be poor in liberty. The gospel proclaims liberty for captives. Think of those unjustly imprisoned, or those in prison for the sake of the gospel. They understand liberty and its value. Behind walls and gates and bolts and bars they have limited rights, few privileges, no voice. Who speaks for those in the prison complex?

And what of the elderly? They have little liberty of movement. Or the disabled? Few pay attention to them. What about the ill? Whatever our success, riches, or fame, we are poor when sickness comes. Jesus' grace was prodigious to the sick. He offered gracious garments of health for those in the tattered garments of illness. By His stripes we were healed. The blows that fell to Him brought us healing. But our society thinks of euthanasia as a cure for suffering – they seek death, not healing, and see no value in suffering.

Others are poor of mind: troubled, broken, psychotic. Our society is marked by mental, emotional, and spiritual brokenness of the highest order. People are tormented by guilt, fear, voices, delusions. They need people to speak for them. Speak up and judge fairly. Defend their rights. Too many end up homeless and on our city streets.

And so many are spiritually needy. They are troubled, twisted, tormented in their imaginations, nerves, body. Think of the wild man of Gadara who was met by Jesus (Mark 5). He was tormented but, after meeting Jesus, Mark says he was "in his right mind." We may not be able to miraculously heal the tormented, but we can speak for them.

Some are needy in spirit. Their faith flags. Their resolve to be faithful falters. Who speaks for them? And what of the seeker? Is there room for them in our lives? Are we patient, available, caring?

And the poor in knowledge; the lost. Do we share our riches with them? And the needy in heart: those who need the softening balm of the gospel. Do we have room for them, and are we generous with pointing them to Christ? John the Baptist wasn't shy with Herod. Nor was Jesus shy with the promiscuous woman at the well, or with corrupt Zacchaeus. He called a traitor, Matthew the tax collector, to follow him.

And there are those who are poor in friends. Jesus, abandoned by his disciples. Think of Paul, abandoned by all his friends except for one: Onesiphorus, who ministered to him when all others gave up on him. He spoke up for Paul. There was Ebed Melech, the Ethiopian, who ministered to Jeremiah when he was friendless, fainting, thirsty, hungry. Jeremiah was rescued from a pit because someone spoke up for him. What about us? Will we be an Ebed

Melech? An Onesiphorus? A faithful Luke? A diligent Timothy? A dear friend, willing to speak up for the good of others?

What about those poor in hope? Do we reach out with human platitudes? Or powerful words of heavenly hope? Do we care for those at our gates or at our feet? The hungry in our communities, the homeless in our streets?

Speak up and judge fairly. Defend the rights of the poor and needy. We live in a world of need, and we are mandated by God to show love to our neighbour. Speak up for those who cannot speak for themselves. Speak up for the destitute, for the sojourner, for the non-citizen, for the non-person. For the pre-born.

PRAYER POINTS

- Thank God for His concern for the poor and needy, and for pointing us to care for them
- Ask for open eyes to see where there are places you can serve and needs you can meet for others
- Remember our history as captive to sin, and thank God for granting you freedom through Jesus
- Ask for courage in speaking up against injustice
- Pray for wisdom in your words and thoughts, that you may speak and judge fairly
- Pray for strength to be a true and loyal friend to the oppressed and voiceless
- Think of local ministries that help the poor, the mentally ill, the homeless – pray that God will use them to enhance His glory, to spread His love and to point people to Him

DISCUSSION QUESTIONS

1. How do we show our concern for the poor, the weak and the needy in our communities? Do we remember those on the fringes and lend our voices and action to their cause?

2. Consider the different kinds of "need" discussed. When you pray for those who are needy, do you also think of the spiritually needy?

3. How can we as a church show we are different in how we care for those within the body of Christ?

4. We are all needy in some way. Do you relate to any of the descriptions above of someone who is poor? How do our own weaknesses help us to serve others and allow others to serve us? How do our weaknesses point us to God?

5. How can we balance truth with grace, confronting sin and sinners in a loving way while never compromising on what the Bible teaches is true? How is doing so part of being a faithful friend?

PSALM 106:34-43

They did not destroy the peoples,
  as the Lord commanded them,
but they mixed with the nations
  and learned to do as they did.
They served their idols,
  which became a snare to them.
They sacrificed their sons
  and their daughters to the demons;
they poured out innocent blood,
  the blood of their sons and daughters,
whom they sacrificed to the idols of Canaan,
  and the land was polluted with blood.
Thus they became unclean by their acts,
  and played the whore in their deeds.
Then the anger of the Lord was kindled against his people,
  and he abhorred his heritage;
he gave them into the hand of the nations,
  so that those who hated them ruled over them.
Their enemies oppressed them,
  and they were brought into subjection under their power.
Many times he delivered them,
  but they were rebellious in their purposes
  and were brought low through their iniquity.

LIFE IS PRECIOUS

JOHN ROKE
Ottawa, 2011

Suggested song: **TAKE MY LIFE AND LET IT BE**
Scripture reading: **PSALM 106:34-43**

Abortion kills a human being. In Canada, approximately 100,000 precious babies are aborted every year. The unborn are the most unprotected human beings in our country - they have no protection. God ordained governments to protect life, to make sure everyone's life is protected, including the lives of the unborn. I don't understand how any person in government called to promote justice and fairness can be so cruel as to not protect the lives of the unborn. We must not be silent when helpless human beings are killed.

How can Canadians be content when virtually all of our federal and provincial leaders allow or favour the abortion of helpless babies who are still in the womb? Though these abortions take place in clinical environments, our land is filled with the blood of unborn children whose lives are precious in God's sight. The land is polluted with blood.

The writer of Psalm 106 tells us that God was disgusted with the people of Israel because they sacrificed their infant children to the idols of their day, such as Molech and Chemosh. The psalmist regarded such sacrifices as sacrifices to demons, an abomination before God. God, the author and giver of life, is never pleased with such sacrifices.

Abortion is not of God - the source of abortion arises from the devil. Jesus said about the devil that he was a murderer from the beginning (John 8:44). Abortion is murder, and as God hates it so should we. God is not pleased with what is happening in our country, and as Christians we need to defend the rights of those who cannot defend themselves.

SACRIFICES OF DEATH

Psalm 106 puts it in these words: "They [Israel] served their idols, which became a snare to them. They even sacrificed their sons and daughters to demons" (verses 36-37). This means that they sacrificed their children in order to appease what they considered gods, or powers, in nature. Their hope was that by sacrificing their own children they would please the gods, who would then grant them rain for their crops, and prosperity when their crops were harvested. They thought they could be richer and more successful if they sacrificed their children to idols.

Of course, we know this was not true. It wasn't idols that had the power to give harvests and prosperity, but God, the true God who created heaven and earth, who grants rain in due season, a God who did not want such sacrifices, and even explicitly condemned them. These sacrifices brought judgment, not blessing!

And what is the main reason for abortions today? Isn't the main reason apparent comfort and ease, or fear of some kind of lack? Children are regarded as an inconvenience, an expense, a stress on finances, relationships, and careers. In other words, people love money and comfort more than they love children. They want to live life on their own terms. There is really very little difference between the ancient practice of infant sacrifice and modern-day abortion.

In verse 38 of Psalm 106, the psalmist adds that, by sacrificing their children, the Israelites shed "innocent blood." The meaning here is not that young children are by nature innocent, but that they were "legally" innocent. They had not transgressed the law of the land. With regard to the unborn, this is all the more true. They are murdered in their mother's womb. Before they can do anything, good or bad, they are killed. Their lives are snuffed out. Psalm 106:38 says that, as a result of what the people of Israel were doing, "the land was polluted with blood." It was polluted with the innocent blood of children. This blood, and the blood of aborted children today, cries out to God for justice.

In the Old Testament laws, if a man in a fight caused the premature birth of a baby by striking a pregnant woman in her stomach, a fine was imposed even if a healthy baby was born. But if the child was maimed, restitution was required: eye for eye, hand for hand, foot for foot. If the baby died as a result of the injury, the man who caused it had to pay with his life (Exodus 21:22-25). This is what God required because an unborn baby is a real human being. He or she is a beautiful and miraculous creation of God, and should be protected.

GOD-GIVEN LIFE

God Himself breathed life into Adam, the first man, and God still does this when a baby is conceived. Each baby is made in God's image. It is His will and power that give breath and life to each human being. Adam exalted the potential birth of children by calling his wife "Eve," or "Chaveh," meaning living. Eve's name means "living" because she would be "the mother of all life" (Genesis 3:20). With the psalmist of Psalm 127 we should exclaim, "Behold, children are a heritage from the LORD, the fruit of the womb a reward" (Psalm 127:3).

It is easy to take away the lives of the unborn, but no doctor can make even one baby live. Only God gives a person life, and only God can rightly take away life. All doctors who do abortions commit murder, and those who permit this are accomplices. Each of us needs to do everything we can to promote and protect life.

There are many people who claim that what develops in the womb is not a real person, only a blob of developing flesh. But friends, this is not what God's Word teaches. It is a child that is in the womb. When an angel tells Mary that her cousin Elizabeth is to have a child, the angel says, "Your relative has also conceived a son in her old age." The child is not an "it," not a blob of tissue. She has conceived a male child! When Mary comes into Elizabeth's home and greets Elizabeth, Elizabeth says to Mary, "When your greeting came to my ears, the baby in my womb leaped for joy" (Luke 1:44). What is in the womb is a baby, a real human being.

At conception, a new human being begins, complete with his or her own unique set of DNA which is present from the first day of life. The new little person's sex is determined from the beginning. About 18 days after conception, the baby's heart is beating. She starts moving 6 weeks after conception, though the mother does not yet feel the movements. At 8 weeks, every part of the body found in an adult is already in the baby. At 11 weeks after conception the baby has growing fingernails. At 12 weeks, the baby's lips open and close. He can wrinkle his forehead, raise his eyebrows, turn his head, smile and frown. At 16 weeks she reacts to sound, sucks and swallows, yawns, stretches, and may get the hiccups. Her toenails, hair, eyebrows and fringe of eyelashes are growing. At 20 weeks, the baby sleeps and wakes and is able to hear. At 24 weeks, the baby may dream and can make a fist and punch it against his mother. This is a busy little person!

As a person, as a real, unique, living human being, fearfully and wonderfully made by God, this child needs our voice and our government's protection.

LIFE IS PRECIOUS

God considered the lives of His people, which includes the lives of the unborn, so precious that He sent His Son to earth to save them. When the Saviour was approached by mothers with their children seeking His blessing, He was clear: "Let the children come to me, for to such belongs the kingdom of God" (Mark 10:13-16).

The Lord Jesus came to give life. Our Lord came not just to enhance temporal lives, but so that many might have eternal life in Him. He came as the innocent lamb of God to give His life for His people. He came so they could have life, and have it abundantly (John 10:10).

We receive eternal life through faith in Him. He blesses His people with the Holy Spirit so that they can come to know Him, and learn to focus on what is most important. When the Lord Jesus Christ, who is the way, the truth, and the life, is recognized as most important, people turn from their sin and evil and place Christ first in their lives. Then they can no longer see the unborn as just blobs of tissue, but as real human beings, and they understand the God-given value of each human being. The pursuit of personal comfort will not be most important; Christ will be most important.

Friends, we need to pray that the hearts of many people will be turned from the way that leads to death and hell, to the living way, the Lord Jesus Christ who leads to life and heaven. We need to pray for hearts to turn so that pro-choice people will turn and become pro-life by faith in Jesus Christ. We must continue to speak, to convince as many as we can that – for their own good, for the good of our communities, and for the good of Canada – it is better to be pro-life than pro-choice. We must continue to show and convince people that the unborn must be protected, that they deserve to be protected because they are fellow human beings.

It is God who creates, who forms babies in their mothers' wombs. It is the government's duty to protect the lives of all Canadians, and it is also our duty to speak up when this is not happening. We must continue to show and convince our government leaders to be pro-life rather than pro-death. We are called to be pro-life, to value and protect the unborn who have been given life by God.

But if you have had an abortion, encouraged someone to have an abortion, or performed an abortion, also know that the God who gives and loves life is merciful. When you repent of your sin, including the sin of abortion, God is faithful to forgive. As God forgives all of us our sins when we come to Him, so God will forgive sins against life, and respond in His great mercy by giving us the hope of eternal life, letting us live not just during this life, but forever.

The life of the unborn is precious in God's sight. The life of the born is precious in God's sight. Life is precious.

PRAYER POINTS

- Pray that Christ may be the most important thing in your own life
- Pray that hearts and minds may be opened to the humanity and value of pre-born children
- Pray for national revival, that more and more people would come to know Christ
- Pray that your local church family would be used as a vehicle to spread revival, and may have courage in speaking up against evil
- Pray for our political leaders, that they may be convicted of their responsibility to protect life

DISCUSSION QUESTIONS

1. How can we as Christians live in a life-honouring way that shows we are different from the world?

2. Read Psalm 127. How can we maintain and promote the Biblical truth that children are a blessing from the Lord? Have you noticed any changes in how Christians view children or large families? How might our culture be impacting us in this regard?

3. Compare the child sacrifice of idol worshippers with abortion. What similarities do you see? Are there differences?

4. How can we condemn abortion and point out its horrors while showing compassion to those who might have had an abortion? Do you think someone in your church who has had an abortion would feel comfortable repenting openly, confident that they would receive love and support from the Christian community?

EXODUS 1:15-22

Then the king of Egypt said to the Hebrew midwives, one of whom was named Shiphrah and the other Puah, "When you serve as midwife to the Hebrew women and see them on the birthstool, if it is a son, you shall kill him, but if it is a daughter, she shall live." But the midwives feared God and did not do as the king of Egypt commanded them, but let the male children live. So the king of Egypt called the midwives and said to them, "Why have you done this, and let the male children live?" The midwives said to Pharaoh, "Because the Hebrew women are not like the Egyptian women, for they are vigorous and give birth before the midwife comes to them." So God dealt well with the midwives. And the people multiplied and grew very strong. And because the midwives feared God, he gave them families. Then Pharaoh commanded all his people, "Every son that is born to the Hebrews you shall cast into the Nile, but you shall let every daughter live."

PRO-LIFE HEROINES: SHIPHRAH AND PUAH

REV. GEORGE VAN POPTA
Ottawa, 2009

Suggested song: **PSALM 128**
Scripture reading: **EXODUS 1:15-22**

The March for Life this year is called "Exodus 2009." Why "Exodus"? When we hear that word, we cannot help but think about the exodus of the children of Israel out of Egypt. This exodus was a good thing. After all, they had ended up as slaves in Egypt. To leave Egypt was a good thing. And yet, the exodus led to a hard time for the children of Israel. It meant forty years in the wilderness, wandering in the deserts of the Sinai Peninsula for years before reaching the Promised Land. During that time, they were often hungry, thirsty, and attacked by marauding nomad tribes.

Canada has been in the wilderness for forty years. We have been wandering with our moral compass spinning around for forty years. What happened forty years ago? Forty years ago, on May 14, 1969, Pierre Elliot Trudeau, the Justice Minister of the day, introduced his controversial "Omnibus Bill" in the House of Commons. The bill called for massive changes to the Criminal Code of Canada. It dealt with issues as diverse as homosexuality, abortion, gambling, gun control, and drunk driving. All these different issues were put into a massive 126-page, 120-clause amendment to our Criminal Code.

And forty years ago, the House of Commons passed this bill. It was a day of infamy for our country because, among other things, it opened wide the door to legal abortion. The bill made it legal for women to have an abortion if a committee of three doctors felt the pregnancy endangered the mental, emotional or physical well-being of the mother. Ever since, our government has sanctioned abortion – the killing of unborn children – on demand.

A VICIOUS COMMAND

I want to draw your attention to a time just before the Biblical exodus, the time when Israel was still in Egypt. The Hebrews, the descendants of Jacob (also known as Israel), had become a large presence within the nation of Egypt. At first, they were treated well because of their connection to Joseph. Joseph, the eleventh son of Jacob, had, through a remarkable series of God-ordained events, become the Prime Minister of Egypt and was the reason the Israelites had found a place in Egypt.

But then a new king arose, a Pharaoh who did not know Joseph. He feared this growing nation of people living within his country. This new king enslaved the Israelite people in order to control them, forcing them to build buildings and cities. He thought that, in this way, he'd keep them under his thumb. But, under God's blessing, the Israelites continued to increase in number. In this context, we are introduced to two remarkable women, Shiphrah and Puah. These women were midwives to the Hebrew women, helping with the births of the Israelite babies.

When slavery and hard labour failed to decrease the Israelite population, the king developed an even more vicious plan. He called the two midwives, Shiphrah and Puah, and told them to kill the baby boys of the Hebrews. At the time of birth, if they saw that it was a little girl, they could let her live. But if it was a baby boy, they were to kill him. Without any boys being born, the Israelite nation would slowly implode.

This plan of Pharaoh, and of Satan, attempted to execute a horrific crime by using the very people that women in childbirth should be able to trust. It's the same strategy used today: if you want to kill babies, the best strategy is to do it behind closed doors of medical clinics, using people in positions of trust, wearing white coats of professionalism.

A FAITHFUL RESPONSE

Shiphrah and Puah, however, disobeyed the king. The text says that "they feared God and did not do what the king of Egypt commanded them to do." You must understand, this took incredible courage! They were risking everything, including their lives, by disobeying this king. But the passage doesn't even mention Shiphrah or Puah's fear of the king. They don't just fear God more than the king – they simply fear God. And that's enough. Everything else falls into perspective.

The Bible teaches that we must obey the government. However, if obeying the civil government leads us to disobey God, we must disobey the government to obey God. Obedience to God always comes first. By obeying the king and killing the boy babies, Shiphrah and Puah would have put themselves in conflict with the commandments of God. They feared God, so they obeyed God; they let the children—girls and boys—live.

The king summoned them and asked them why all these baby boys were living. Why had they not killed them? They answered, "Hebrew women are not like Egyptian women; they are vigorous and give birth before the midwives arrive." And then we read that the Lord blessed Shiphrah and Puah for their faithfulness. Because they feared God, He gave them families of their own.

Shiphrah and Puah could not stop the evil king - he then gave the order that every boy born to an Israelite woman was to be thrown into the Nile River. They could not stop the evil, but they stood up for what was right and did what they could in the role God had given them. They did what was right because they feared God. These two women risked their lives and livelihoods in order to save innocent babies.

A FAITHFUL SAVIOUR

When we hear about a king killing baby boys, our minds go from that moment in history to another moment, another king who killed baby boys: the wicked King Herod the Great (Matthew 1). When King Herod heard from the magi that a king who was Christ the Lord was born in Bethlehem, he sent his soldiers to kill all the baby boys aged two and under in Bethlehem. An angel warned Joseph and Mary to escape—to go, of all places, to Egypt.

And so Jesus, the Saviour of the world, was saved alive. He would come back from Egypt, grow into a man, live a perfect life, and eventually die on the cross for the salvation of all who look to Him in faith, all who confess their sins and trust that they are forgiven for Jesus' sake. There is forgiveness for Jesus' sake. That includes forgiveness for those who commit the sin of abortion.

This Jesus died, but rose again. He ascended into heaven, and He is coming again, coming as the judge of all people.

Today there is so much crime, so much injustice, so much cruelty. We are contemplating just one example of injustice here—abortion. But we are in the wilderness, waiting on God's timing. We know that Jesus will set everything right. Just like the Yeshua of the Old Testament led Israel from the wilderness into the Promised Land, so the Yeshua of the New Testament – Jesus – will lead us from this present wilderness into the heavenly Promised Land.

In the meantime, He calls upon us to do what is right. We do not wait in blissful passivity doing nothing because, well, Jesus is going to make everything right. No. We are called to act. Let us be inspired by Shiphrah and Puah, two women who stood up for life, who held the line for the babies. Shiphrah and Puah are pro-life heroines. They defended and promoted life. Let us do the same, in honour and memory of Shiphrah and Puah, and in obedience to God.

PRAYER POINTS

- Thank God for the example of Shiphrah and Puah's courage and faithfulness, for preserving their names and story as an example for us
- Pray that your fear of God would always be stronger than your fear of men
- Pray for wisdom for our government, and for discernment about when to obey and when to take a stand against their direction
- Pray for the return of Jesus to make everything right; Come Lord Jesus, Maranatha!
- Pray that those suffering after an abortion would know forgiveness in Jesus Christ, would confess their sins to Him and find freedom from guilt and shame
- Thank God for a forgiveness that covers all sins, and bring your own sins before Him

DISCUSSION QUESTIONS

1. Shiphrah and Puah risked their lives and livelihoods to save babies. What kinds of things might you risk – money, reputation, career, social standing, entertainment – in order to protect lives and take a stand against abortion?

2. When Shiphrah and Puah are called back to Pharaoh, they lie about the reason for the baby boys' survival rate. We know that lying is wrong, yet this is recorded for us in connection to God's blessing on the midwives for their actions. How do you explain this?

3. This story is an example of being called to faithfulness in our daily tasks. How do you show faithfulness to God in your work?

4. Read Romans 1:16-17. How does this apply to how we respond to assaults on the gospel from the government, or from colleagues, family members, or friends who ask us to do things we know go against the will of God revealed in His word?

ISAIAH 5:1-7

Let me sing for my beloved
　my love song concerning his vineyard:
My beloved had a vineyard
　on a very fertile hill.
He dug it and cleared it of stones,
　and planted it with choice vines;
he built a watchtower in the midst of it,
　and hewed out a wine vat in it;
and he looked for it to yield grapes,
　but it yielded wild grapes.
And now, O inhabitants of Jerusalem
　and men of Judah,
judge between me and my vineyard.
What more was there to do for my vineyard,
　that I have not done in it?
When I looked for it to yield grapes,
　why did it yield wild grapes?
And now I will tell you
　what I will do to my vineyard.
I will remove its hedge,
　and it shall be devoured;
I will break down its wall,
　and it shall be trampled down.
I will make it a waste;
　it shall not be pruned or hoed,
　and briers and thorns shall grow up;
I will also command the clouds
　that they rain no rain upon it.

For the vineyard of the Lord of hosts
 is the house of Israel, and the men of Judah are his
 pleasant planting;
 and he looked for justice, but behold, bloodshed;
 for righteousness, but behold, an outcry!

PSALM 139

To the choirmaster. A Psalm of David.

O Lord, you have searched me and known me!
You know when I sit down and when I rise up;
 you discern my thoughts from afar.
You search out my path and my lying down
 and are acquainted with all my ways.
Even before a word is on my tongue,
 behold, O Lord, you know it altogether.
You hem me in, behind and before,
 and lay your hand upon me.
Such knowledge is too wonderful for me;
 it is high; I cannot attain it.
Where shall I go from your Spirit?
 Or where shall I flee from your presence?
If I ascend to heaven, you are there!
 If I make my bed in Sheol, you are there!
If I take the wings of the morning
 and dwell in the uttermost parts of the sea,
even there your hand shall lead me,
 and your right hand shall hold me.
If I say, "Surely the darkness shall cover me,

and the light about me be night,"
even the darkness is not dark to you;
  the night is bright as the day,
  for darkness is as light with you.
For you formed my inward parts;
  you knitted me together in my mother's womb.
I praise you, for I am fearfully and wonderfully made.
Wonderful are your works; my soul knows it very well.
My frame was not hidden from you,
when I was being made in secret,
  intricately woven in the depths of the earth.
Your eyes saw my unformed substance;
in your book were written, every one of them,
  the days that were formed for me,
  when as yet there was none of them.
How precious to me are your thoughts, O God!
  How vast is the sum of them!
If I would count them, they are more than the sand.
  I awake, and I am still with you.
Oh that you would slay the wicked, O God!
  O men of blood, depart from me!
They speak against you with malicious intent;
  your enemies take your name in vain.
Do I not hate those who hate you, O Lord?
  And do I not loathe those who rise up against you?
I hate them with complete hatred; I count them my enemies.
Search me, O God, and know my heart!
  Try me and know my thoughts!
And see if there be any grievous way in me,
  and lead me in the way everlasting!

SEEK JUSTICE AND RIGHTEOUSNESS

JOHN VAN POPTA
Ottawa, 2008

Suggested song: **PSALM 139**
Scripture reading: **ISAIAH 5:1-7, PSALM 139**

In Isaiah 5, Isaiah tells the people of Israel how God looked at His vineyard, at the people He had planted, and instead of seeing justice and righteousness He sees bloodshed and outcry. Isaiah's indictment of the people in Chapter 5:7 is worded for dramatic effect: the words for "righteousness" and "cry" sound nearly alike, as do the words for "justice" and "bloodshed." "God looked for Mishpat but saw mishpach; for tsedikah but heard tse-akah."

Isaiah's play on words pierces to the truth of the matter. What the world calls justice – justice for women, for society, for community – is in fact bloodshed. What the world defines as righteousness –

apparent acts of equality and empowerment – is heard by God as a crying out.

We too see this lack of justice and righteousness. We look for righteousness in the House of Commons and the Senate, but we find none. We go past the Supreme Court buildings seeking justice for our smallest neighbours, but find only bloodshed. We live by buildings that symbolize righteousness and justice, places where laws are made and upheld. In these places things are supposed to be right, but they are not.

We need to cry out over this bloodshed. We need to give voice to those whose distress is silent. We know that God hears the silenced cries, because He knows the inmost thoughts of all those He has created, even before they are born. Psalm 139 speaks to us in profound ways in a day and age when God is not considered much. We serve an awesome God. This is a day and age when the word "awesome" is used to describe hockey players, or a delicious dinner, or just about anything else, but not God. We live in a time when webcams make it possible for you to see almost anywhere, anytime, and where the internet makes information available to anyone, anytime. We live in a world where holiness and righteousness are words that mean little. What's holy except cows? What's "justify" except the way to make your margins straight?

But Psalm 139 reminds us of our human limitations, and teaches us that it is only God who sees all, who is everywhere, all the time (verse 7). He is everywhere you might try to be. He is powerful. He created you and knew every day of your existence before you ever came to be (verse 16). He is familiar with everything about you. He is without peer or rival. There is none like Him (verses 6, 17).

We see God's almighty power and attributes, and then in the same psalm we have hard words: slay the wicked (verse 19). I hate those who hate you (verse 21). And then follows submission: search me, know me, test me, lead me (verse 23-24). Let's reflect on these words of Psalm 139.

KNOWING GOD

This psalm is known for its description of the all-seeing God. God is searching, searching for you. It began with Adam and Eve. They sinned, and God called out to them in their hiding place: "Where are you?" He knew where they were. But still He called for them. And He does that to you today. Jamie, Kevin, where are you? Jasmine, Katie, where are you?

As David says, we must say: "Lord, you see everything about me. You see me when I get up in the morning and head out to school. You see me when I go home and go to bed. You see me when I'm with my friends or family. You're familiar with all my ways."

Familiar with all your ways. Is that a good thing? What do you think? Does that make you feel good, or scared? Comforted, or uncomfortable? Just think about it. God does not need a webcam aimed at a few places in the world so He can check up on you. No, He is familiar with all your ways. What you do, where you go, how you speak. How you feel about that is a reflection on your lifestyle. God knows everything about you, what you do, where you go, even your thoughts. What do you think about that?

We also read that God is all-present, that He is everywhere. He knows everything about you, and He is there with you. When you rise, when you sleep. You can't get away from Him. The highest heavens, the farthest distance on earth, the deepest cave – even death itself is no place of escape! And why can't you escape Him? Because the Lord God made it all. He is the creator.

So, David begins to reflect on that. Not only has everything around him been created by God, but he is personally God's creation! God is the all-creative God. Biology can tell you much, but there is a mystery in life that can't be figured out. Somehow in a mother's womb a child is conceived, grows, and matures and develops into a newborn child. Knit together in a mother's womb. Fearfully and wonderfully made. Before you were born God knew everything about you. What do you think about that? Is that comforting, or does it make you uncomfortable?

This knowledge of God should be comforting. Even through death and the grave, your heavenly Father will not leave you. In our lives, difficulties come. You already know that. Times of sorrow, sickness, disease, distress, even death. But God is in absolute control. He is without peer or rival. And so, we can say with David, "How precious to me are your thoughts, O God" (verse 17).

How precious! Like a jewel to be held, to be admired, to be treasured. When we read the Word of God, our heavenly Father gives us access to His thoughts. In the Scriptures, we have the thoughts of God. Have you ever thought of that before? In the Bible you can learn and discern something about the mind of God. We can take those words, those thoughts of God, and turn them as we would a precious gem. A diamond on an engagement ring. Reflecting on the wonders of creation, the power of God, or the intricacies of the human body, should cause us to marvel. How precious, how precious are your thoughts, O God.

As we reflect on this psalm, we also realize that God is the all-holy God. A holy God who knows everything about us. About me. He knows the words of my tongue before they are formed. The days of my life, before they began. Knew of my body, before it was formed. His thoughts are too wonderful for me. He knows of my sins and my sinfulness.

This can make us feel guilty, unworthy to approach this holy, powerful God. But wow, He won't leave me in the grave because He loves me. Because He loves me and in Jesus Christ gave His life for me, I too can be made holy. Isn't that marvellous? We look forward to the great and glorious day of Jesus Christ because of what He has accomplished for us.

STANDING WITH GOD

In verse 19, suddenly the mood of Psalm 139 changes: "Slay the wicked O Lord. I hate them." We wonder, why is this in this psalm? Well, this is also about the holiness of God.

As we marvel at the everywhere-present God, as we are astonished at His greatness, as we are awed by His power, so we are stunned by His holiness. Holy means "set apart." God says to you, "You are holy." That means you are set apart. Separated and distinct. When we say that God is holy, we say He sets Himself apart. If we set something apart, we tend to move it away from the centre. But when God sets apart, He moves things together, to the centre.

In the centre is God. And so, in setting us apart, He moves us to be with Him, in the centre. In Christ we are in the centre. There are those in the world who are wicked and bloodthirsty, who have evil intent. There are those who misuse God's name and rise up against the holy, all-powerful, all-seeing creator God, who want to move God and His people away from the centre and put themselves in that place. This is why David says, "Those who are against you, O Lord, well, I'm against them too. I know whose side I'm on."

These strong words are not words of spite. These words are founded on an understanding of the greatness and holiness of God. Knowing the holiness of God – His goodness, His power, His righteousness – makes evil intolerable. We must stand against all that stands in opposition to God. We must hate what He hates.

We know that our thoughts are an open book to God. Many of His thoughts and ways are incomprehensible to us, but He understands absolutely everything about us. And yet, despite this difference between us, we can know Him. We can be filled with awe and a sense of divine mystery. We acknowledge that our little minds are baffled by the infinite mind of God. And we can say with the apostle Peter in John 21:17, "Lord, you know all things; you know that I love you."

In loving God, and in recognizing His divine power, we then submit to His searching, and we commit to hate evil, and with Him to seek righteousness and justice. "You have searched me God," the psalm begins. "You know me." It ends with, "Lord, search me." Lord, know me. Test me. Prove me. Help me to hate what you hate, to stand with you for what is right. Your thoughts are precious to me, and I want to be led by you in the way everlasting. Knowing who God is and who we are, we can be comforted, for we can know that, with Jesus Christ, God has taken us and put us with Him in the centre, where we are safe. There He leads you and me in the way everlasting. He leads us to glory.

We look for justice, but instead there is bloodshed - for mishpat, but there is mishpach. We search for righteousness but hear cries of distress - for tsedikah, but there is tse-akah. Let us stand up for the sake of justice for the unborn, for the disabled, for the elderly. Let us seek righteousness in the land. We know that God, who sees and knows all, who is holy and powerful, is also the One who can move nations and peoples to repentance. He has done it before. He can do it again. There will be justice and righteousness in His land.

PRAYER POINTS

- Pray for justice and righteousness in our land, a turning to God and a hatred of sins, including the sin of abortion
- Praise God for His all-seeing, all-creative, all-knowing, all-holy character
- Seek forgiveness for hidden sins, thoughts and actions you'd prefer no one knew about, and ask God to search and know you
- Read through Psalm 139 as a prayer

DISCUSSION QUESTIONS

1. Do you sometimes adjust your behaviour based on who is physically present in the room with you? When and why would you be more likely to do this? Do you hold others to account for their behaviour around you?

2. How does it impact you to meditate on the truth that God sees and knows every one of your thoughts and actions? Do you find it comforting or uncomfortable to think about God's searching of you?

3. Things have not changed much since the days of David and the days of Isaiah. How can we faithfully seek and promote righteousness when we are surrounded by bloodshed?

4. How do we show that we are set apart in the world, holy to God?

PSALM 14

The fool says in his heart, "There is no God."
  They are corrupt, they do abominable deeds;
  there is none who does good.
The Lord looks down from heaven on the children of man,
  to see if there are any who understand,
  who seek after God.
They have all turned aside; together they have become corrupt;
  there is none who does good,
  not even one.
Have they no knowledge, all the evildoers
  who eat up my people as they eat bread
  and do not call upon the Lord?
There they are in great terror,
  for God is with the generation of the righteous.
You would shame the plans of the poor,
  but the Lord is his refuge.
Oh, that salvation for Israel would come out of Zion!
  When the Lord restores the fortunes of his people,
  let Jacob rejoice, let Israel be glad.

JAMES 1:19-27

Know this, my beloved brothers: let every person be quick to hear, slow to speak, slow to anger; for the anger of man does not produce the righteousness of God. Therefore put away all filthiness and rampant wickedness and receive with meekness the implanted word, which is able to save your souls.

But be doers of the word, and not hearers only, deceiving yourselves. For if anyone is a hearer of the word and not a doer, he is like a man who looks intently at his natural face in a mirror. For he looks at himself and goes away and at once forgets what he was like. But the one who looks into the perfect law, the law of liberty, and perseveres, being no hearer who forgets but a doer who acts, he will be blessed in his doing.

If anyone thinks he is religious and does not bridle his tongue but deceives his heart, this person's religion is worthless. Religion that is pure and undefiled before God the Father is this: to visit orphans and widows in their affliction, and to keep oneself unstained from the world.

BOTH HEARERS AND DOERS

MARC JAGT
Ottawa, 2007

Suggested song: PSALM 146
Scripture reading: PSALM 14, JAMES 1:19-27

Each year, over 50 million lives are taken worldwide through abortion. In Canada, it's around 100,000. There are about 330,000 live births each year, so that means about one child in every four is killed before he sees the light of day. Who can talk about that as if these are just "numbers?" In Canadian law, there's a massive hole in the area of protection for these pre-born children. Our law is given to protect rights and freedoms – but there's nothing to protect the rights of the smallest humans. Section 223 of the Criminal Code says that a child only becomes a human being when it has completely exited the mother's body - even if it has not yet breathed! Somehow it is just this change of location which changes a child from a non-person just before birth to a legal "human being" just after birth.

Coming face to face with this atrocity is a Herculean task. Acknowledging the evils of racism or slavery are one thing, though they too are no little things. But for a society to acknowledge and take responsibility for the fact that it has put to death hundreds of thousands of its own – that seems humanly impossible. What reaction are we to have to this evil? It is easy to "see red" on this – easy to rant and rave. But Christians are called to make a greater response to evil. We are called to lead the way, to be teachers, to show by our own example what our society needs to do.

LET'S FIRST OF ALL GRIEVE

Let's grieve for our society, when it is unable or unwilling to do so for itself. And let's grieve more deeply than it wants to as well. What we see in society's support for abortion is nothing less than fundamental rebellion against God, the same rebellion instigated by the devil in the very beginning. Abortion activists shout things like "Get your laws off my body," or "My body, my choice." We hear a cry for autonomy, a demand for self-rule: "Get your laws off my life." When we hear that we should hear the ancient rebellion that lives in our own hearts as well: "Get your laws off my body" is what we all tell God when we sin. The sin of abortion is my sin, your sin, as well. It must be grieved.

Here we see sin's true colours. All sin is a rejection of God – His authority, His ways – and all sin brings death. Our society would have you think that you and I can be islands, places where decisions can be made that are purely our own and do not affect others. But that is a lie. All of our thoughts and words and actions have consequences.

And abortion makes it very clear: despite what we may tell ourselves, everything that is anti-God is anti-life.

In Psalm 14 the psalmist talks about practical atheists, those who say in their hearts that "there is no God." The psalmist goes on to describe their life: "They eat up my people as they eat bread." Those who deny God will trample others, destroy them. All sin does this, and all sinners do this. The fool who denies God does not pray, but he preys. Practical atheists become pirates, looters, and not-so-innocent bystanders. Did you know that Joseph Stalin was trained as a minister before he fiercely rejected the faith? He went on to kill more than 15 million of his own people during his brutal rule in the Soviet Union.

C.S. Lewis, in his book *The Abolition of Man*, makes it clear that society needs to turn to God and be built upon Him. Morality, good and evil, can only be established, founded, in God. Everything else will be a building on sand. If you abandon the Creator, you will neglect, or destroy, the creature as well. In fact, respect for life, all human life, is a thoroughly Christian concept. And that's so clear around us today, as our society tries to move further and further from God, and we see the consequences. So, let's recognize what is going on in the world. This evil is even darker and deeper than it looks at first. And it's an evil that exists in my heart, and yours as well.

WHAT ARE WE THEN TO DO?

Let's make it clear, first, that we are to do something. Too often religion is used as a way of escaping from the world rather than a way of ministering to it. We can satisfy our own taste for spirituality but neglect to care for those around us. In the Book of James, we are called to be doers of the word, not just hearers. We are called to help widows and orphans. In fact, James says this practice of our faith is the essence of religion: "Religion that is pure and undefiled before God the Father is this: to visit orphans and widows in their affliction, and to keep oneself unstained from the world."

The Hebrew word for 'widow' in this text comes from a root word meaning 'silent,' or 'unable to speak.' Widows at that time had no voice or standing in the culture, and were often taken advantage of by others. God's people were not exempt from this tendency to trample on the vulnerable. Read through some of the Old Testament prophets as they called the people to repentance time and time again – the Israelites went into exile for this failure to care for each other! James tells us this needs to be at the heart of our faith: to give a voice to those who have no voice, to care for those who seem to be of no use to us or to others.

Why? Because that is where we were and such grace was shown to us – abundant grace. We had no rights, no voice, before God – yet He reached down in love to redeem and save us. The essence of Christianity is extending help to those who cannot help themselves! This is not a task for a special few – it was a call to all of Israel, and remains a call for the church today. Are not the unborn among the most vulnerable and voiceless in our society?

If we can save even one life, or make even one person think twice about abortion, it is worth speaking up. Maybe you have heard the story of the stranded starfish. A man went to the beach and saw that, after a storm, the sand was littered with thousands and thousands of stranded starfish. A small boy was walking among them, throwing something into the water. When the man got closer, he saw that the boy was picking up starfish and throwing them back into the sea. The man pointed out that there were probably tens of thousands of starfish on that beach and his efforts probably wouldn't make a difference. The boy picked up another starfish, threw it into the sea, and replied, "It made a difference for that one."

May we have that spirit of hope, that willingness to put in major effort for "minor" results, that commitment to small acts of faithfulness. May we not give in to overwhelm or feelings of uselessness, but instead work faithfully in the small things and trust God with the results, because we know what He has already accomplished for us.

In the beginning of the world, blood was shed. Abel was killed by his older brother Cain (Genesis 4). Sin so clearly brought death. And Abel's blood cried out from the ground. The LORD God heard that blood! And He hears the voice of all the blood that is shed today as well, crying out from the ground. But things do not stop at the blood of Abel. Other blood has been shed, that of Jesus Christ. "You have come to Jesus, the mediator of a new covenant, and to the sprinkled blood that speaks a better word than the blood of Abel" (Hebrews 12:24). This blood speaks of grace and forgiveness; this blood means life and restoration. This blood proclaims that justice will not be the last word.

There is no Band-Aid solution for the problem of evil in this world, or for the injustice of abortion. It is beyond fathoming. Who can deal with the atrocities of this dark world? Only Jesus Christ! He entered its absolute darkness. He suffered hellish agony on the cross. He is the way forward, the way of life and hope. Only in Him do we find something greater than our evil and the evil around us. May the ugliness of evil bloodshed lead us all to the healing blood of the Lamb.

PRAYER POINTS

- Praise God for His perfect righteousness and pray for a better understanding of right and wrong so that you can be angry for the right reasons
- Seek God's intervention on behalf of your country, praying for freedom to speak up and receptive hearts softened by the Spirit
- Pray for a spirit of hope, and ask for God's strength in fighting feelings of being overwhelmed by the sin and evil so prevalent in the world
- Thank God for His authority, for giving us a light burden and easy yoke. Ask for a heart willing to submit to His authority and pray for someone you know who has rejected God's authority in their life
- Pray that your government (local and federal) would recognize God's authority and govern accordingly
- Pray for widows, the lonely, the poor, and the chronically ill. Ask God to show you ways to minister to them

DISCUSSION QUESTIONS

1. Do you sometimes feel overwhelmed by the scope of problems in the world (not just abortion, but also other issues such as wars, poverty, hunger, climate change, etc.)? Do you tend to think you cannot make much of a difference? How can you change that perspective? What small acts of faithfulness can you do to make a difference?

2. Read Jeremiah 22:1-5, Ezekiel 22:6-7, and Matthew 23:23-24. Are we in danger of forgetting or trampling on the vulnerable, as the Israelites and Pharisees did? Now read Acts 6:1-7. How do we care for the vulnerable as church today?

3. How does pride impact our relationship to God as the higher authority? Do you struggle to submit to God's will and think you might know better what would be best for you?

4. In James 1:26 we read: "If anyone thinks he is religious and does not bridle his tongue but deceives his heart, this person's religion is worthless." Discuss how our words can reflect our religion either poorly or well, and how we can speak with both grace and truth.

GENESIS 3:1-6

Now the serpent was more crafty than any other beast of the field that the Lord God had made. He said to the woman, "Did God actually say, 'You shall not eat of any tree in the garden'?" And the woman said to the serpent, "We may eat of the fruit of the trees in the garden, but God said, 'You shall not eat of the fruit of the tree that is in the midst of the garden, neither shall you touch it, lest you die.'" But the serpent said to the woman, "You will not surely die. For God knows that when you eat of it your eyes will be opened, and you will be like God, knowing good and evil." So when the woman saw that the tree was good for food, and that it was a delight to the eyes, and that the tree was to be desired to make one wise, she took of its fruit and ate, and she also gave some to her husband who was with her, and he ate.

PSALM 82

A Psalm of Asaph.

God has taken his place in the divine council;
  in the midst of the gods he holds judgment:
"How long will you judge unjustly
  and show partiality to the wicked?
Give justice to the weak and the fatherless;
  maintain the right of the afflicted and the destitute.
Rescue the weak and the needy;
  deliver them from the hand of the wicked."
They have neither knowledge nor understanding,

they walk about in darkness;
all the foundations of the earth are shaken.
I said, "You are gods,
  sons of the Most High, all of you;
nevertheless, like men you shall die, and fall like any prince."
Arise, O God, judge the earth;
  for you shall inherit all the nations!

ROMANS 1:16-25

For I am not ashamed of the gospel, for it is the power of God for salvation to everyone who believes, to the Jew first and also to the Greek. For in it the righteousness of God is revealed from faith for faith, as it is written, "The righteous shall live by faith."

For the wrath of God is revealed from heaven against all ungodliness and unrighteousness of men, who by their unrighteousness suppress the truth. For what can be known about God is plain to them, because God has shown it to them. For his invisible attributes, namely, his eternal power and divine nature, have been clearly perceived, ever since the creation of the world, in the things that have been made. So they are without excuse. For although they knew God, they did not honor him as God or give thanks to him, but they became futile in their thinking, and their foolish hearts were darkened. Claiming to be wise, they became fools, and exchanged the glory of the immortal God for images resembling mortal man and birds and animals and creeping things.

Therefore God gave them up in the lusts of their hearts to impurity, to the dishonoring of their bodies among themselves, because they exchanged the truth about God for a lie and worshiped and served the creature rather than the Creator, who is blessed forever! Amen.

FOUNDATIONAL ISSUES

MARC JAGT
Ottawa, 2006

Suggested song: **PSALM 82**
Scripture reading: **GENESIS 3:1-6, PSALM 82, ROMANS 1:16-25**

What do these two examples have in common?
- Emperor Qin Shi Huang of China, credited with implementing a massive new road system and getting the Great Wall of China built, effectively unifying and protecting the nation.
- A 1939 decision in Germany, signed by Hitler, to engage in "mercy killings" of those deemed incurably sick. Strong economic and compassionate reasons were given.

In both cases, the leaders were hailed as doing good - great good. They seemed to advance the well-being of their nations. But there was so much more going on.

Emperor Qin Shi Huang built a strong nation, but also banned and burned books, buried scholars alive, and killed anyone who failed to please him. He lived in fear of death and evil spirits. He spent almost 40 years building his own grave, ensuring he was buried with thousands of soldiers to protect him. You breathe a sigh of relief when you discover he replaced live soldiers with clay models - until you learn he was, in fact, actually buried with the women from his harem and his palace staff.

In Germany, Hitler used the cloak of war against other nations to mask the war that was instigated upon the weak and vulnerable of Germany's own people. More than 250,000 people were killed in these involuntary euthanasias, which targeted the mentally ill and disabled. How ironic that Hitler himself eventually lost everything that he had assumed was his to take and responded by committing suicide.

There are times and situations where a society's true colours can be seen – if you have the eyes to see. Once you get past the rhetoric, the glory of a prosperous and secure empire, the propaganda of terms like "showing mercy," there is far more than meets the eye. There is an old saying that "The road to hell is paved with good intentions." Behind great evil is often great reasons for it – reasons that look and sound good and decent, and so are hard to recognize for the evil they are. It is crucial to look deeper.

LOOK AT THE FOUNDATION

We can see the same story playing out today. Sadly, there is more to our beautiful nation of Canada than what you might see at first glance. While our society claims to be about freedom, prosperity, and a commitment to human rights, we know there are evils lurking under the surface that do not support those ideals. Something is terribly wrong at the foundation.

Abortion is one of the telltale evils lurking below the surface in Canada. As a nation we knowingly sanction murder behind closed doors, cloaking it in euphemisms and language about "choice" and "rights." But if we have the eyes to see it, we will see evil on full display here. It is shocking and undeniable.

And how are we, as Christians living in this nation, to respond?

Through the lens of the Word of God, we have a unique understanding of the foundational issues in society. We recognize the primal sin that is foundational to evil: our own desire to be gods unto ourselves. In the Garden of Eden we, at the devil's instigation, threw off the authority of God. We demanded the "knowledge of good and evil" – which, in Biblical language, is specifically the desire to determine what is good and evil. As sinners, we want to do what is right in our own eyes, and look out only for ourselves. We believe there is freedom in autonomy, including moral autonomy.

Our darkened minds do not understand the foolishness of these thoughts, and the serious consequences that accompany them. For our first parents, the consequence was a broken relationship with God that affected all of humanity. For God, the consequence was the death of His only Son.

We need to confess: we cannot be God. We do not and cannot establish morality. Without God, there is no justice or morality to follow, so pragmatic arguments are the only ones that make sense. In this setting, ends justify means and contribution determines value. It is only belief in God that protects the weak and helpless. It is only belief in God that results in servant-hearted leadership. Ultimately, it is only belief in God that can save our nation.

Without God, why would new life, or any life, be sacred? Under a pragmatic belief system, why should life be protected? We can argue with our neighbours until we're blue in the face about the unique humanity of each pre-born child, but if they have no basis to believe in the sanctity of life, they have no reason to stand up for pre-born children who are at risk of being murdered.

A DEEPER PROBLEM

This leads us to the deeper problem, the large and dangerous base of the iceberg. Sin is not just a physical problem, it is much more – it is mental, philosophical, and deeply spiritual. From the beginning, man has attempted to suppress the truth by wickedness, believing that declaring there is no God will make it so. People who live this way essentially put their fingers in their ears, not wanting to hear truth. Consciences are deadened by repeated, unrepentant sin.

Sin is the reason abortion exists, and sin is the reason the foundation of our nation is unstable. Abortion is a symptom of a much deeper cultural problem: a prevailing belief that we are in control, and that we have a say in life and death. Abortion is an even greater evil than we think. It not only takes the lives of innocent children, it devalues God-created life as a whole. Abortion is a slap in the face of God, ungratefully throwing His good gift of life away.

We need more than a law restricting abortion – we need a Saviour! Every one of us individually needs a Saviour, one who has conquered sin and death, who puts God back on the throne in our lives, and who actually is in control. We need to test ourselves, to make sure our trust is not in ourselves and our illusions of control.

And our leaders and our neighbours need this same Saviour. Divine power and grace have the power to change hearts and minds, to stabilize the foundation of a nation.

As Christians, we are called to represent God's valuing of human life as the crown of His creation. Our worth is in Him, not in any status conferred on us by our government. And we live in hope, because we know God has done something greater than any human leader can do. He is the God who acts, and He will deal with the full depth of injustice, not just the surface. He will deal with evil, and He will do it in ways we least expect – the cross shows us that. He will display His glory and remove evil in a wonderful way. May the blood of abortion lead people to the blood of the Lamb, and may He be pleased to use us in this fight for the foundation of our nation.

PRAYER POINTS

- Rejoice that God is greater than the greatest evil, and has won the victory
- Express your grief over the evil of abortion and ask for hearts to be softened to the beauty and value of all human life
- Humbly confess your sin as no different from the sin of abortion, a rebellion against God
- Pray that the efforts of abortion activists would be thwarted, while pro-life efforts grow and succeed
- Pray for wisdom for Christians on the front lines of the abortion issue: politicians, activists, doctors and nurses
- Pray for courage to live not as a passive bystander, but as an active Christian willing to face persecution for the glory of God

DISCUSSION QUESTIONS

1. What do people base their morals on if they do not believe in God? How can we see society changing because there is no shared belief in a set truth about good and bad?

2. Reflect on the fact that the most powerful leaders do not find peace or joy in their position, their authority, or their wealth. How does this point us to God? How can it encourage us to pray for our leaders?

3. Think about our culture's desire for autonomy and independence. List some ways God reminds us that we are finite (for example, our need for sleep), and that we are created for relationship, not to be islands all alone.

4. Does it help grow your compassion to focus on your own sin as being a rebellion against God, an act of unfaithfulness? How does humility help us to be better pro-life activists?

5. We tend to pray for solutions we can think of, yet God often moves in surprising, unexpected ways. Think of Biblical examples where God acted in a way no one would expect, or using a person we would never expect. Have you seen similar examples in your own story of faith?

EPILOGUE:
A MODEL OF DETERMINATION

by **TIM CHALLIES**
Suggested song: **LO, WHAT A CLOUD OF WITNESSES**

This message was originally given at the Reformed March for Life prayer service in Ottawa in 2014, and subsequently published on www.challies.com in 2016. It is reprinted here with permission.

I want us to travel together into the past, to England in the late 1700s. King George III is on the throne, though this is before the madness that would mark his final days. The Industrial Revolution is well underway and life is changing as people begin a great migration to the cities to pursue those new factory jobs. On the other side of the Atlantic, the American colonies have recently declared their independence.

Let's zoom in on the year 1789 and the city of London. A well-dressed man walks into the British parliament and he delivers a daring speech. He makes a bold proposal. He wants to bring an end to a great evil, an evil he believes is staining his entire nation.

At this time in history, England is a nation that not only allows slavery, but actually condones and supports it. In fact, the English economy has come to depend on it. British ships are constantly sailing down the African coast, and as they go they are capturing men, women and children and shipping them across the Atlantic into a life of slavery. Countless thousands of these slaves will die along the way. Families are ripped apart; women are treated savagely; children are torn from their parents. These slaves are regarded as less than human, unworthy of rights and freedoms. North American plantations are producing vast wealth and making England a rich nation, but only at this cost—the cost of allowing and advocating slavery. Slavery is so much a part of the economy that almost nobody believes that anything can ever change.

But one man does. One man believes he can make a difference. His name is William Wilberforce. Wilberforce had become a Member of Parliament in 1780 when he was only 21 years old. Five years later, he experienced a great change in his life when he read a Bible and came to believe that he was a sinner who needed to be saved by Jesus Christ. That experience forever transformed his life and now, just four years later, he has come to see slavery as a great and reprehensible evil and he will dedicate his life to ending it. He believes that whether a person has dark skin or light skin, whether he was born in Africa or England, all are equally created in the image of God. All human beings have equal dignity and worth because all are equally made in the image of the Creator. None has the right to enslave another.

Epilogue: A Model of Determination

And so, this man stands in front of his fellow members of Parliament and makes a speech in which he pleads justice for slaves and he proclaims that slavery is immoral, it is wrong. He is being very strategic here. He is not proposing that slavery be done away with all together. Not yet. There will be time for that. First, he simply proposes that the slave trade be regulated and curtailed. Yet even this modest proposal is defeated. The vote is not even close.

He is defeated and slavery continues. Those ships continue to steal thousands and thousands of people and take them far away. But Wilberforce will not stop fighting. He will not go away. He brings bills forward again in 1791, 1792, 1793, 1797, 1798, 1799, 1804, and 1805. And every time he is defeated. He is defeated by filibuster. He is defeated by illness. He is defeated by unrest and rebellion among slaves. He is defeated by international interests that simply refuse to allow the slave trade to die. He is defeated by plain old bigotry.

But still he does not give up. He does not surrender. His enemies come up with a strategy: If we can destroy the man, we can destroy the cause. So, they try to destroy him. Even when great personal attacks come against him, even when people try to destroy his name and reputation, he persists. He fights on.

Much later, Wilberforce reflects on this time and says, "So enormous, so dreadful did the slave trade's wickedness appear that my own mind was completely made up for abolition. Let the consequences be what they would: I from this time determined that I would never rest until I had effected its abolition."

His first success comes in 1807, almost 20 years after he first began his crusade. In this year, his persistence leads to a bill to abolish the slave trade in the British West Indies. Now, suddenly, the slave trade is illegal. This does nothing for those who are already slaves, but it is a start—an important start.

And a better day, too, will come. Wilberforce will live to see the triumph of his cause when slavery is finally and completely abolished. He is a man who changed the world by staying committed to his cause, by staying committing to his principles, by staying committed to what he knew God had called him to do.

We look back on William Wilberforce today and see his life and times as a great triumph of good over evil. Rightly do we regard him as a heroic figure. But his life was one of constant battles and discouragement. The one great victory came only after many, many crushing defeats. It was his persistence that changed minds, that changed his nation, that changed the course of history. If he had grown weary, if he had lost his confidence in his cause, he would not have rewritten history. He would not have been the hero he is today.

William Wilberforce exemplified one great but rare characteristic, one great but rare Christian trait. He was a model of determination. A model of persistence. A model of perseverance as he pursued what he knew God had called him to do. God had given him a desire and an opportunity and he persisted until he had completed the work God had called him to.

**Sources: *Amazing Grace: William Wilberforce and the Heroic Campaign to End Slavery* by Eric Metaxas (2007); *William Wilberforce: A Hero for Humanity* by Kevin Belmonte (2007).

PRAYER POINTS

- Thank God for surrounding us with such a great cloud of witnesses, for heroic Christians who stand as examples for us today
- Pray for courage and persistence in the face of opposition or defeat
- Pray for a strong community and good friends who will encourage and build you up, who are willing to work alongside you for the kingdom
- Pray that the hearts of more politicians may be changed as Wilberforce's was, to make them champions for God in their positions of influence

DISCUSSION QUESTIONS

1. Brainstorm texts that can help in times of discouragement. What verses can you memorize to point you back to God's sovereignty and His delight in your faithfulness regardless of the outcome? (See for example Colossians 3:23.)

2. We are often quick to get on board with a cause when we see a need for change. But sometimes we try to do something, fail, and then think "Oh well, we tried. We did what we could." How can we better practice persistence and determination? How can living and worshipping in community help?

3. Wilberforce was a politician before he was a Christian, but becoming a Christian changed everything about how he did his job. How is your daily work impacted by your love for Jesus and commitment to God's kingdom?

4. What issues in society today are similar to slavery in Wilberforce's day? What culturally-accepted evils do we need to persistently, constantly speak up against no matter what the consequences?

APPENDIX: PRAYERS

In some ministers' sermon notes, full prayers were included. These prayers are a continuation of their message, and are included here with permission. May they guide and encourage you in prayer to the God who hears and answers, and who has the power to change hearts, change minds, and save lives.

PRAYERS 1 - 3
(WINSTON BOSCH)

A PRAYER FOR THE SUFFERING AND THE SELFISH

Lord Father in heaven, God of all comfort, we pray in the name of Jesus that you would bring comfort, safety and security to suffering women in our country. We pray for those women mistreated and abandoned by men, pushed into pregnancy and then into abortion. Lord, stop evildoers and abusers in their tracks. Be a friend to the oppressed. Give suffering women the allies they need and surround them with loving support, also the loving support of the church, so they can make good, life-giving decisions. We ask for your mercy on women who are feeling trapped, mercy for those feeling like their only option leads them to an abortion clinic. Lord, protect women from all the manipulative truth-bending abuse of the anti-woman abortion industry here in Canada. Protect their minds and hearts from those who sell murderous solutions that turn women against their own children. And Lord, be a God of great comfort to all those women who have aborted their children but have taken refuge in you. Remove the shame and guilt from their lives by the costly blood of your own Son. Help them to know in a deep and real way that they and their children belong, body and soul, in life and death, to their faithful Saviour Jesus Christ.

And as we pray for the suffering, we also pray for the selfish. Lord, we hate sin. We hate sin in our own lives, we hate selfishness in our own lives, and in the lives of others. And we hate the selfishness that leaves dead babies in its wake. We pray that you would put a stop to the work of those who have bought and now sell the lie that personal convenience trumps children's existence. Lord, have mercy on the souls of those whose hearts are darkened and minds are filled with the futile lies that personal comfort and ambition is justification for the killing of unborn children.

Lord open the eyes of the spiritually dead so that they might see life! Open the minds and hearts of the selfish, that they may see a Saviour and be called to repentance and sorrow over sin. Open our mouths to speak grace and truth like Jesus. Lord, bring an end to abortion. We know that only you have the power to end this injustice. May justice roll on like a river and righteousness like a never-failing stream. Lord, come to judge the living and the dead. And Lord have mercy; O Lord have mercy on us all. Amen.

A PRAYER FOR STRENGTH TO LIVE A SACRIFICIAL LIFE

Lord Jesus, we come to you knowing we stand in the shadow of your cross. Thank you for your example of sacrifice, your sacrifice that overcomes our sins. Fill us with your Spirit, cause us to have the same mindset as Christ: to love as you love, to forgive as you forgive, to be conformed to the pattern of your life and death, to live lives of sacrifice as you did Lord, to follow in your footsteps and so show others to you.

Lord, this world oozes with suffering and selfishness. May your church rise to greet it with the open arms of sacrifice. Forgive us where we have bowed our own knee to the idols of comfort and convenience. May we offer our whole lives as living sacrifices. Teach us in the school of the good prostitute.

We offer you our hearts and homes, our minds and lives, promptly and sincerely. We pledge to you and your kingdom our time, our money, our reputations, our plans, our comforts. May we be found opening our homes, not hiding in them. May we be found building bigger tables, not higher fences. May we be found putting more chairs around our kitchen tables, opening our families to care for the children you grant us, and also to foster and adopt children, to house and help pregnant women who need somewhere to stay. And for those of us who cannot do so, may we support those who can.

Help us to learn from the good prostitute, that we would yearn that children would live, that we would cry: by no means put the child to death! Lord God, then back our cry with our own willingness to give and live sacrificially. Lord, bless, encourage, and strengthen the brave men and women who choose life against difficult circumstances. Bless, encourage, and strengthen us to be brave, to pray and work for the sanctity of life with Christ-like sacrifice today and every day of our lives. Amen.

A PRAYER FOR GOVERNMENT

O Lord, you have given the government the sword to exercise justice, not to execute children. So we cry out in your name, Jesus, that you would give our government an understanding mind to govern our country rightly. Give them wisdom to discern between the good and evil. Lord, may our government leaders protect the suffering, the vulnerable, the dependent, the voiceless and the powerless, wherever they are, and whatever size they are. Move mightily O Lord! Work through faithful pro-life elected leaders, work through faithful Christians advocating for light and life. May we see in our day incremental change, and may we see in our lifetime wholescale change. Lord, be merciful and gracious to us as a nation, so that we may one day hear Parliament recognize the pre-born child as a human being and make abortion illegal.

Lord Jesus, give us hope. May we praise you, the King of kings and the Lord of lords, you who are far greater than Solomon. We praise you as you give us hope through the advancement of your kingdom and the promise that the gates of hell shall not prevail against it and that you are coming to judge the living and the dead. Thank you that, in the end, life will win over death, that the Saviour will save the suffering, that sacrifice will overcome selfishness, that you will wipe every tear from every eye, that you will vindicate the oppressed and give us the living hope that you, O King, will see to it that abortion will be no more, for you are making all things new. Maranatha, come Lord Jesus. Amen.

PRAYER 4

(BEN SCHOOF)

O Lord God we praise you for your perfections. We have seen from your word how you are all-knowing, omniscient. You have searched us and you know us. And this means that you have a personal, intimate relationship with us. This knowledge is too wonderful for us, because it is hard to believe that you, a holy God, would want to have a personal relationship with us.

Your great creative power is seen in your beautiful creation, especially in each of us as human beings. You take such good care to fashion us perfectly in our mother's womb, you build us by hand. What love, what care can be seen in each person you have created. We praise you because we are fearfully and wonderfully made. Your works are wonderful, we know that full well. How precious are your thoughts to us, O God. How vast is the sum of them!

And so, we pray for the wicked, for those who do not acknowledge you, who think they can run away or hide from you. Particularly we think of the bloodthirsty men and women who do not respect the sanctity of life. We think of those who murder, or defend the murder of the unborn, who rip apart the life that you have woven together, as well as those who promote the murder of the elderly, the sick and anyone else society does not consider worthwhile. These crimes grieve us – we hate them and even those who perpetrate them, and we pray that you will bring justice soon. Bring justice for the murdered little ones, for the elderly, and for all innocent blood shed. We know that you see each injustice and that you will bring perfect justice.

But Lord, we also pray for the salvation of the sinner. We know that no one is beyond the reach of your salvation. And we know that we are not innocent either. Search us, O God and know our heart. Test us, to know our anxious thoughts. Reveal any offensive way in us. We know that were it not for your work in us and your salvation in Christ we would be just as wicked. We are no better by nature, so forgive us our wickedness through Christ. We pray also for those who have obtained abortions and repented. Thank you that there is forgiveness in Christ: His blood is powerful enough even to cover murder. Help your children struggling with this to seek, receive, and feel your forgiveness.

Grant us boldness today and always to fight, to protest, to work to end the horror of abortion. Though we are angry, help us also in our conduct today to show the love of Christ. And lead us in the way everlasting. Amen.

PRAYER 5
(PETER H. HOLTVLÜWER)

Our Father in heaven,

We praise you for the gift of life and for sending us the Lord of life, Jesus Christ your Son. What a great and gracious Saviour He is—going to great lengths to convert one lost soul, overcoming the power of the evil one with but a word, and restoring him to life and peace. We thank you for rescuing us, too, from our enslavement to sin and Satan and taking us into your holy family. All of this is something we don't deserve but which you nevertheless give in your love.

Lord Jesus, ascended on high and seated at the throne of your Father, work mightily in the hearts of our fellow Canadians who at this moment are blinded by the evil one. Send forth your Spirit to change the thinking that prevails today and to turn around a culture that is lurching toward death and which is mired in despair. Rescue people trapped in an existence without rhyme or reason or purpose and show them the better way, your way. Open their eyes to the love of their Creator who made each human being in His own image, who has given worth and value to every life, young or old, weak or strong. Let them come to know you, Lord Jesus, as Saviour and King, and receive the gift of life, eternal life at your right hand.

Bless the March for Life, that it may be an instrument to raise awareness in our country for the cause of the unborn. Be with every expecting mother and give to each the instinct to protect and nurture life. Bless those who help struggling, single mothers, and those who take in foster children and who adopt children whose biological parents are unable to raise them. May we as Christians be at the forefront of giving such help, as a reflection of our Saviour and His love for the life He helped create.

Strengthen us with grace and arm us with truth as we bring your message to an often-hostile world. Reduce their hostility, Father, and in its place work receptivity in the hearts of all who hear the message of life today.

In the Name of Jesus Christ we pray,

Amen.

www.ingramcontent.com/pod-product-compliance
Lightning Source LLC
Chambersburg PA
CBHW072151100526
44589CB00015B/2179